OSPREY AIRCRAFT OF THE ACES • 16

Spitfire Mark V
Aces 1941-45

SERIES EDITOR: TONY HOLMES

OSPREY AIRCRAFT OF THE ACES • 16

Spitfire Mark V Aces 1941-45

Dr Alfred Price

OSPREY
AEROSPACE

Front cover
Flg Off Neville Duke of No 92 Sqn
breaks off combat with a cluster of
Ju 87B-2/Trops after having
successfully 'flamed' one of the eight
Stukas engaged by his unit on the
afternoon of 21 January 1943 south
of Tripoli – he was flying Spitfire Mk
VB ER220 on this occasion. Duke
recounted this action in his classic
autobiography, *Test Pilot*, first
published in 1953;

'During our first show over this
area with 12 Spitfires at 18,000 ft, we
saw some Ju 87 Stukas returning
from bombing our troops. I reported
them to our wing leader, Wg Cdr
Darwen, and dived down on them
with the squadron following.

'I felt rather exposed approaching
the formation of Stukas on my own
and for a time, until the squadron
arrived, I had them all to myself,
returning my fire and doing stall
turns around me. They were Italian
Stukas (it has since been established
that they were in fact Luftwaffe
aircraft from III./StG 3, Ed.) and I
caught up with them near Castel
Benito aerodrome at about 1000 ft.
I shot at one without doing much
damage but hit a second one in the
starboard wing root, saw it burst
into flames, spiral down and explode
when it hit the ground'
(*Cover artwork by Iain Wyllie*)

First published in Great Britain in 1997 by Osprey, an imprint of
Reed Books Limited, Michelin House, 81 Fulham Road, London SW3 6RB
Auckland and Melbourne

ISBN 1 85532635 3

Edited by Tony Holmes
Page design: TT Designs, T & S Truscott
Cover Artwork: Iain Wyllie
Aircraft Profiles: Keith Fretwell
Figure Artwork: Mike Chappell
Scale Drawings: Mark Styling

Printed in Hong Kong

EDITOR'S NOTE
To make this best-selling series as authoritative as possible, the editor would
be extremely interested in hearing from any individual who may have relevant
photographs, documentation or first-hand experiences relating to the elite
pilots, and their aircraft, of the various theatres of war. Any material used
will be fully credited to its original source. Please write to Tony Holmes at
1 Bradbourne Road, Sevenoaks, Kent, TN13 3PZ, Great Britain.

For a free catalogue of all books published by Osprey Aviation please write to:
Osprey Marketing, Reed Books, Michelin House, 81 Fulham Road,
London SW3 6RB

CONTENTS

AUTHOR'S INTRODUCTION

The Spitfire Mk V bore the brunt of RAF fighter operations during the difficult period between the end of the Battle of Britain and mid-1943, when the Allied air forces were finally able to assert full technical and numerical superiority over their enemies. The hardest fights involving Mk Vs were those staged over Malta. To get even a small batch of these fighters to the island was a major undertaking involving an aircraft carrier to transport them half way, followed by a 600-mile ferry flight to complete the journey. Once there, the fighters, and their pilots, were thrust into a life-and-death struggle against larger enemy forces. For several months it was touch-and-go whether the island would be bombed or starved into submission, but in the end the defenders prevailed.

With Malta's needs met, Spitfire Vs could be sent to more-distant battle fronts. Wherever they went, their arrival boosted the morale of those they had come to defend. More tangibly, within weeks of entering action in Egypt and South-East Asia, they brought a measure of air superiority to Allied forces that had suffered because of the lack of it. Only during operations in the defence of northern Australia in spring/summer 1943 did the Mk Vs fail to live up to the high expectations placed on them.

After the Mk V had been superseded as a high altitude fighter through the arrival of the Mk IX in the autumn of 1942, the variant took on a new lease of life fitted with a Merlin engine optimised for low altitude operations – as late as the summer of 1944, the Spitfire LF V equipped several frontline fighter squadrons assigned to home defence.

This account concentrates on the ace pilots credited with five or more aerial victories. In listing pilots' credited victory scores, only confirmed claims are considered – unconfirmed kills have been omitted, as have claims for aircraft destroyed or damaged on the ground.

A number of good friends contributed material and photographs to assist with the preparation of this book, namely Norman Franks, Dilip Sarkar, Philip Jarrett, Andrew Thomas, Wojtek Matusiak, Stephen Fochuk and Bruce Robertson – I proffer my grateful thanks to you all. At the same time Ted Hooton made available his painstaking and extensive research into Spitfire V modification states. This proved of great assist in enabling profile artist Keith Fretwell to produce accurate colour plates of the aircraft flown by the various aces, and scale drawing artist Mark Styling to create the most accurate plans of the Mk V yet seen in print.

Last, but by no means least, I wish to express my gratitude to Chris Shores for allowing me to use material from the superb reference books he has co-authored over the years, namely: *Aces High, Malta - The Spitfire Year* and *Fighters Over Tunisia*. The first volume in this short list is the standard reference work on RAF aces during World War 2, while the second two books hold this status regarding the actions they describe. I am also grateful to Chris for making available the results of the combined research effort undertaken by himself, Brian Cull, Ian Primmer and Yasuho Izawa, in Japan, into Japanese air attacks on northern Australia.

Alfred Price
January 1997

STOP-GAP SPITFIRE VARIANT

During the winter of 1940/41 a major main concern of Air Chief Marshal Sir Sholto Douglas, C-in-C Fighter Command, was that he would have to re-fight the Battle of Britain the following spring. In the previous year the RAF's intelligence service had learned much about the Luftwaffe, although large areas of uncertainty still existed. One of these concerned its adversary's policy regarding the next generation of combat aircraft. There had been numerous reports and rumours of new fighter and bomber types with enhanced high altitude performance under development in Germany. Already the diesel-engined Junkers Ju 86P reconnaissance aircraft, which could flying at altitudes exceeding 36,000 ft, had demonstrated that it could operate over Great Britain with virtual impunity. If the Luftwaffe initiated large-scale attacks using bombers with this capability, the RAF's current fighter types would be unable to meet such a threat. These fears would prove to be unjustified, but at the time they had a profound effect on Spitfire development.

The variant originally intended to replace the Spitfire Mks I and II in production was the Mk III, which boasted a re-engineered and strengthened airframe incorporating several design improvements. Converting production lines to build the Mark III would involve considerable re-tooling, however, and that would take time. Supermarine made it clear that it could not guarantee to meet the tight production schedule for the new variant demanded by the RAF.

Another source of difficulty in getting the Spitfire III into production concerned its engine, the Merlin XX, which featured a redesigned supercharger with two separate blowers – one for high-altitude and the other for low-altitude operation. It was a complicated engine, and Rolls-Royce stated that it would be difficult to build in sufficient quantities in the

Mk VBs of the initial production batch awaiting collection from Eastleigh in April 1941. These aircraft would go first to No 6 Maintenance Unit at Brize Norton for fitting of the cannon and other items of operational equipment. W3127, the aircraft nearest the camera, had a very full career. After serving with Nos 74, 401, 340, 453, 222, 167 and 316 Sqns and the Central Gunnery School, it became an instructional airframe in 1946 (*via Sarkar*)

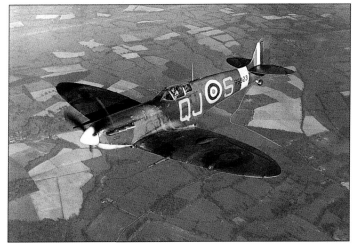

Top and above
One of the first Mk VBs produced, R6923/QJ-S was converted from a Mk IB and issued to No 92 Sqn in early 1941. The aircraft was the personal mount of Flg Off Alan Wright, who ended the war credited with 11 and 3 shared enemy aircraft destroyed, 5 probably destroyed and 7 damaged

required time. A short-term solution to the problem was near at hand, however.

In parallel with the Merlin XX, Rolls-Royce produced a simplified variant of the engine with the low altitude blower deleted. This engine, christened the Merlin 45, developed 1515 hp at 11,000 ft at +16 lb boost, and being devoid of the second blower, was considerably easier to mass-produce than the Mk XX. Moreover, although it was no larger and little heavier than earlier Merlin variants, the Mk 45 gave a sizeable increase in power.

Thanks to its physical similarity to the Mk XX, the new engine could be fitted to Spitfire I and II airframes with little modification. This variant was designated the Spitfire Mk V, and Rolls-Royce received instructions to convert 23 Mk Is to the new standard. Most of those converted in that initial batch were cannon-armed Mk IBs, although there were also a few Mk IAs fitted with all-machine-gun armament.

During January 1941 the first Mk Vs appeared, and initial flight trials revealed that the variant offered most of the performance advantages of the Mk III, but without the predicted delays in bringing the latter into production. During a planning conference in early March, the Chief of the Air Staff (CAS), Air Chief Marshal Sir Charles Portal, sounded the death knell for the Spitfire III. The minutes recorded;

'CAS has decided that the Spitfire V with Merlin 45 engines with single-speed blowers shall be put into production instead of Spitfire IIIs. The Spitfire V with improved Merlin 45 (with a slightly larger blower impeller – i.e. the Merlin 46) will give better performance in altitude and ceiling. This will meet the needs of Fighter Command for high altitude fighters. If the type is a success the Air Staff will want as many as can be produced.'

Despite the wording of the final sentence, other contemporary documents make it clear that the Air Staff regarded the Mk V as a stop-gap expedient. The definitive high-altitude interceptor was to be the Spitfire VI, which was now under development at the highest priority. Essentially this aircraft was a Mk V fitted with a pressurised cabin, a larger wing and a new version of the Merlin with a yet more powerful supercharger. As soon as the Mk VI was ready it was to replace the Mk V on the production lines.

No 92 Sqn at Manston, flying Spitfire IBs and commanded by fighter ace Sqn Ldr John Kent, was selected as the unit to introduce the Mk V into service, the first converted Mk IB (X4257) arriving at the squadron in the middle of February 1941. In the weeks that followed, the unit sent a succession of its Spitfire IBs to the Rolls-Royce plant at Hucknall for conversion to Mk VB standard. The work appears to have taken about a week to ten days to complete, after which the re-engined fighter was returned to the unit. As a result of this protracted change-over, for several weeks No 92 Sqn flew both marks operationally.

Because of the procedure outlined earlier, the first Mk Vs were almost all VB variants armed with two 20 mm cannon and four .303-in machine guns (the rest were Mk VAs armed with eight machine guns).

Externally, the first Mk Vs were almost identical to late-production Mk Is and IIs, but this changed when pilots found that the Merlin 45 ran at excessively high oil temperatures and correspondingly low pressures when at high altitude. The oil cooling system was not powerful enough to meet the increased demands now made upon it, so a larger matrix had to be fitted to the cooler, which in turn required a larger intake to provide an increased flow of air through it. Thus, the oil cooler intake under the port wing of the Mk V was enlarged and made circular (instead of semi-circular as on the Mks I and II), giving a clear identification feature for the new variant. The change was incorporated on new aircraft on the production line, and was carried out retrospectively to all previously converted Mk Vs.

Fighter Command was keen to bring the new Spitfire into action over occupied Europe as soon as possible, but it suddenly faced objections to this from an unexpected quarter. On 28 February Prime Minister Winston Churchill minuted his CAS;

'It would be a mistake I think to exhibit the Merlin 45 or the Merlin 45 plus (the Merlin 46) to the enemy till there are at least half a dozen Squadrons capable of using them. Certainly they should not be used over the other side without further instructions.'

As a result of the stress associated with his position, Churchill would sometimes make ill-considered decisions, and this was one such case. Yet one of his strengths as a war leader was that he would allow reasoned arguments to persuade him to change his mind. Three days later Sir Charles Portal replied, setting out in detail his opposition to the ban;

'I have issued instructions that the Spitfire V is not to be used in circumstances involving risk of capture by the enemy until at least six squadrons are equipped with the type.

Sqn Ldr James Rankin, (left, without jacket) OC No 92 Sqn, and Flt Lt Charles Kingcome are pictured here 'lighting up' on their return from an operation over France early in 1941. Full details of Rankin's career are given in chapter eight. Charles Kingcome went on to command No 72 Sqn and, later, the Kenley Wing. At the end of the war his victory score was 8 and 3 shared destroyed, 5 probably destroyed and 13 damaged

'I should nevertheless be grateful if I could be told the reason for this decision since it is not one which I should have recommended, and the A.O.C.-in-C Fighter Command is opposed to it.

'My reasons against the decision are:-

(a) there is nothing in the Merlin (45) which the Germans could themselves make use of with advantage in the near future.

(b) There is nothing new for the pilots to learn in the way of tactics and handling of the aircraft, such as might justify the holding back of an entirely new type of fighter until we were ready to spring an effective surprise on the enemy.'

Portal pointed out that about two months would elapse before the required six squadrons were re-equipped with the new Spitfire variant. In the interim, an increasing proportion of the more dangerous sorties would be flown by units operating earlier variants of the fighter. That might have an adverse effect on the morale of pilots. As a separate issue the ban would prevent the use of the new engine fitted in photographic reconnaissance Spitfires, which were flying missions into Germany and relied on their speed to survive. Portal ended his minute with the request;

'If in the light of the above information if you would reconsider your decision I should be very grateful.'

On 7 March the Prime Minister replied. He said he had wanted to wait until the new variant could be used in sufficient numbers to strike a really effective blow, and cited the premature use of tanks in action during the previous war. Yet he ended his minute with the reply Portal had sought;

'However, if you think it (the immediate use of the Merlin 45-powered Spitfires over enemy territory) a good thing to do, I shall certainly not contest your opinion.'

The matter was closed, and Fighter Command could send its Spitfire Vs over occupied Europe as soon as it felt ready.

Although the entry of the Mk V into service went off relatively smoothly, there were hiccups. On 19 March 1941 No 92 Sqn had three Spitfire VBs crash-land in quick succession without a single shot being fired at them by the enemy. The doomed flight, led by Sqn Ldr James Rankin, having been sent on a long, and fruitless, chase to engage Messerschmitts on an offensive sweep over Kent at 36,000 ft in newly-converted Mk VBs R6776, R6897 and X4257.

The cause of the losses was attributed to the failure of the constant speed unit (CSU) controlling the fighters' de Havilland Hydromatic propellers. Normally the CSU limited the maximum speed of the Merlin engine to about 3000 rpm, but at the very low temperatures encountered during this sortie the oil in the CSU congealed, the propeller blades went to full fine pitch and the engine rpm raced uncontrollably to around the 4000 mark. With the engine threatening to shake itself to pieces, the pilot had to shut down

Hero worship. Air Training Corps cadets gaze on in awe as Sgt Donald Kingaby of No 92 Sqn tells what it was like to fly the Spitfire in combat. The 11 victory crosses under the windscreen suggest the photo was taken in the spring of 1941. By war's end Kingaby had been credited with 21 and 2 shared destroyed, 6 probably destroyed and 11 damaged

Groundcrewman swarm over a Mk VB of No 485 'New Zealand' Sqn at Redhill in August 1941, carrying out a rapid refuelling and re-arming between sorties. Note the partially empty boxes of .303-in ammunition in the centre foreground, and the 20 mm drum magazine at the right foreground (*via Scutts*)

immediately. All three fighters made crash-landings and their pilots escaped without injury, although the aircraft incurred enough damage to keep them out of service for several months. Following this incident, pilots flying the Mk V at extreme altitude were ordered to make frequent throttle changes to exercise the propeller pitch mechanism, whilst as many Spitfire Vs as possible were fitted with Rotol constant-speed units until a modification was developed to cure the problem.

During March 1941 the dispersed production facilities controlled by the Supermarine Company terminated production of the Spitfire I in favour of the Mk V and went on to turn out 38 examples of the latter. Twelve of the new aircraft were Mk VBs, the other twenty-six being Mk VAs. In April (the first full month of production of the Mk V) 58 examples were produced – 36 Mk VAs and 22 Mk VBs.

During the course of that same month, No 92 Sqn came to full strength with Mk VBs the use of both converted Mk IBs and new-build aircraft. The next in the queue to receive the new variant was No 91 Sqn at Hawkinge, the Channel coast unit completing the change-over during the first week of May.

The new Spitfire variant became operational at almost exactly the same time as the Bf 109F-2, the latter aircraft being an extensive redesign of the famous German fighter, boasting a cleaner aerodynamic shape than its predecessors. The 'Friedrich-2' had a maximum speed of 373 mph at 19,700 ft and a service ceiling of 36,100 ft – figures that were remarkably close to those of the Spitfire VB (see the appendices for more performance details). Low down the new Messerschmitt fighter was the superior aircraft, being some 27 mph faster than the Spitfire V at 10,000 ft and having a better rate of climb.

In terms of firepower the Spitfire VB was the better armed, its two 20 mm cannon and four machine guns giving it a more powerful 'punch' than the single 15 mm cannon and two 7.9 mm machine guns fitted to the Bf 109F-2. Overall, in the types of action where they would meet, the Spitfire V and the Bf 109F were more or less equally matched, and the near technical parity that had existed between the Spitfire and the principal German fighter type in 1940 would continue for some time to come.

In the months following the appearance of the Spitfire V, the war situation underwent a series of far-reaching changes that imposed new tactical requirements from the RAF fighter force. To meet these demands Supermarine engineers were kept hard at work devising a stream of modifications to improve the performance of the Spitfire. Many were fitted to new aircraft on the production lines, whilst others were incorporated at modification and repair centres. In the next chapter some of the more important changes are examined, and the effect they had on the aircraft's fighting capability.

IMPROVING THE BREED

During the service life of the Spitfire V more than 1100 modifications were devised for this variant, with the majority of these being incorporated in at least some of the production aircraft. The changes ranged from the major to the relatively minor. For example, Modification 411 introduced a whole series of so-called 'tropicalisation' changes necessary to enable the fighter to operate effectively in desert-type conditions, whilst Modification 536, by contrast, was relatively simple and involved the fitting of an improved locking catch for the cockpit canopy. Below are described some of the more important changes made to the Spitfire V.

Below and bottom
In July 1941 the huge plant production facility at Castle Bromwich, outside Birmingham, began turning out Mk Vs in large numbers. These photos show production at full swing at the plant during 1942 (*Vickers*)

— METAL AILERONS —

Once Spitfires engaged in high speed combat it was found that at speeds above 400 mph the ailerons seemed to lock solid, with pilots needing to use all their strength to get any movement in the rolling plane – they lost many firing opportunities as a result. When pilots started to complain, the cause of the problem was soon isolated. At high speed the airflow caused the fabric covering on the ailerons to balloon out, thus raising the stick forces necessary to move the control surface. The answer was to replace the fabric covering with one of light alloy, as the latter was stiffer and did not balloon at high speed.

Repairs in progress on Mk VAs and Bs, as well as a few Mk Is, at the Westland Aircraft Ltd plant at Ilchester in January 1942. Aircraft AD313, just visible above the wings in the left foreground, carries the badge of No 317 (Polish) Sqn behind the cockpit. The next aircraft along in the left-hand line is W3841, which carries a cartoon dog painted under the cockpit. Damaged in combat while flying with No 501 Sqn, this aircraft later went on to serve with Nos 72 and 121 Sqns before it was lost in action on 16 June 1942

In November 1940 Battle of Britain ace Sqn Ldr A V R 'Sandy' Johnstone, then OC of No 602 Sqn, test flew a Mk I fitted with the new ailerons and found a considerable improvement in the fighter's high speed handling. He described the flight in his autobiography *Enemy in the Sky* (William Kimber 1976);

'Geoffrey Quill (Vickers-Supermarine test pilot) flew in again with another modification for us to try out. This time it was a Spitfire fitted with metal ailerons which, when I flew the machine, turned out to be a big improvement over the fabric-covered version. I found it to be much lighter and more positive on the controls. Finlay (Flt Lt Finlay Boyd, who was also a Spitfire ace) tried it out later and confirmed my opinion, so we have told Geoffrey we would like to buy some!'

At the time Johnstone stated in his official report on the flight that 'The effectiveness of the new ailerons is so great that one has to fly the aircraft to believe it . . .'

During 1941 Supermarine ran a crash programme to fit metal-covered ailerons to frontline Spitfires, pilots bringing their aircraft to Eastleigh to have them modified on a 'while you wait' basis. It took some months for production of the new ailerons to catch up with demand, however, and it was not until the late spring that sufficient numbers had been manufactured to fit them to all Mk Vs on the production line.

— MERLIN IMPROVEMENTS —

The Merlin 45 engine fitted to the first Mk Vs had a 10.25-in diameter supercharger blower, which gave the fighter a full-throttle altitude of 13,000 ft and saw the aircraft achieve its maximum speed at 18,000 ft. The Merlin 46, on the other hand, was optimised for higher altitude operations with its larger 10.85-in diameter blower giving the Mk Vs a full-throttle altitude of 15,200 ft. This engine gave the fighter its maximum speed at 24,000 ft. At all altitudes above 20,000 ft the Mk V with the Merlin 46 was faster than a comparable fighter fitted with the Merlin 45 – the maximum speed advantage was 7 mph at 28,000 ft.

One problem that dogged the Spitfire during manoeuvring combats

Mk VBs of No 243 Sqn, which formed at Ouston in June 1942. The aircraft nearest the camera, EN821, was delivered new to the unit as part of its initial complement. It later served with No 65 Sqn until December of that same year, when it was damaged in a flying accident. After repair, it was turned over to the Royal Navy and ended its days as an instructional airframe at Lee on Solent air station (*via Jarrett*)

Close-up of the later-type bulged canopy fitted to the Mk V, which gave the pilot improved vision to the rear

early on in the war was its inability to sustain manoeuvres involving negative G. Under those conditions the Merlin's float-type carburettor ceased to deliver fuel, and if the pilot held the manoeuvre the engine would splutter to a stop. When he ceased applying negative G, initially there was a further problem for the excess of fuel in the upper part of the carburettor produced an over-rich fuel/air mixture in the cylinders, which caused a drop in power for a few seconds before normality returned.

Most engines fitted to Luftwaffe combat types, by contrast, had direct fuel injection and so were immune from this failing. German pilots soon learned that when chased by a British fighter, a bunt followed by a high speed dive was usually enough to shake any assailant off – many a German aircraft escaped destruction by using this tactic.

Several schemes were tried to solve this problem, but in the end Beatrice Schilling, a scientist working at the Royal Aircraft Establishment at Farnborough, devised a clever, but relatively simple, change to the SU carburettor fitted to the Merlin. Her so-called 'anti-G' modification was subsequently fitted to the Merlin engines which powered the later Spitfire Vs.

SPITFIRE MK VC

The initial production versions of the Spitfire V, the Mk VA and VB, involved merely the installation of the Merlin 45 engine into airframes of Mk Is and IIs. However, the extra weight of the new engine, armament and additional equipment left little reserve of strength in these airframes to allow for future development. The Mk VC featured a redesigned and strengthened airframe and other refinements, and production began in October 1941. This version was fitted with the 'C-Type', or 'Universal', wing, which had provision to accommodate an armament of eight .303-in machine guns, two 20 cannon and four machine guns, or four 20 mm cannon only.

EXTENDING THE RANGE

With the requirement to send Spitfires to Malta (see Chapter Four) came the urgent need to extend the fighter's ferry range. The only feasible method of delivering Spitfires to the besieged island was to carry them half way by aircraft carrier, at which point pilots would then complete a deck launch and fly the rest of the way. However, that still meant a flight of about 660 miles had to be completed, which was far in excess of the fighter's range on internal fuel only.

To make the flight possible, Supermarine developed the jettisonable 90-gallon slipper tank which would fit under the Spitfire's fuselage. This device more than doubled the fighter's fuel capacity, and aircraft earmarked for the reinforcement operation were modified to carry and draw fuel from the new tank.

Following the successful use of the ferry tanks, slipper tanks were

also produced in 30- and 45-gallon sizes for use during combat missions, and these were used in all theatres where the Mk V went into action. The largest, and most remarkable, ferry tank of them could carry 170 gallons of fuel, this veritable monster hanging below the fuselage just a few inches off the runway. With the 170-gallon tank further supplanted by a 29-gallon cell in the rear fuselage, the Spitfire V could fly the 1100-mile trip from Gibraltar to Malta in a single hop.

Engine fitters lower a Merlin 46 into position in a Mk VB on the Castle Bromwich production line in August 1942. No fewer than ten different variants of the Merlin were fitted to versions of the Mk V that saw service with frontline units (*via Vickers*)

TROPICAL MODIFICATIONS

The Spitfire required special modifications to enable it to operate successfully in overseas theatres, foremost among these being the fitting of a filter to the carburettor air intake to prevent dust and sand entering the engine and causing excessive wear. Without such a filter, the running life of the engine was greatly reduced. The first such filter unit was housed in a large beard-like fairing under the nose, but this modification was not popular with pilots for it reduced the ram-effect of the air entering the carburettor air intake, and thus reduced both the fighter's maximum speed and its rate of climb. Later, engineers at No 103 Maintenance Unit at Aboukir, Egypt, built a smaller and more efficient type of filter unit for installation in the Spitfire. Nicknamed the 'Aboukir Filter', it was fitted to most Mk Vs operating in North Africa.

Other changes made to Mk Vs modified for tropical operations included the following items stowed in the fuselage behind the cockpit: tank for $1^{1}/2$ gallons of drinking water; container for flying rations; emergency tool roll; and additional emergency equipment, including heliograph mirror, ground-signalling strips, signal pistol and cartridges.

——— EFFECTS OF MINOR MODIFICATIONS ———

In 1943 Mk VB EN946 was employed at Farnborough in a series of tests to determine the effect of minor modifications to improve performance. The effects of the changes were as follows:

Maximum speed of fighter initially	357 mph
Fitting multi-ejector exhausts instead of 'fish-tail' type	7 mph
Removal of carburettor ice guard	8 mph
Fitting rear-view mirror with improved fairing	3 mph
Whip aerial in place of mast-type	$1/2$ mph
Cutting the cartridge case and link ejector chutes flush with the wing	1 mph
Sealing cracks, rubbing down, painting and polishing wing leading edge	6 mph
Wax polishing the remainder of the aircraft	3 mph
Maximum speed of fighter with all changes incorporated	$385 1/2$ mph

Together, these individually small changes to the aircraft increased the speed of the aircraft by $18 1/2$ mph, which was enough to make a considerable difference in combat. Conversely, small deteriorations in the airframe could combine to give similar reductions in performance. Sand or dust adhering to patches of leaked oil, dents or scratches (most critically on the wing leading edge to about one-third back), or repaired battle damage could reduce the fighter's maximum speed to below that of the standard machine.

——— OPTIMISED FOR LOW ALTITUDE OPS ———

As previously stated, the Merlin 45 and 46 engines were optimised for high altitude operations. To permit operations at low altitudes these engines had an automatic boost control unit (ABCU) to prevent overboosting, which could cause pre-detonation and possible damage to the cylinders – the same went for the Spitfire IX fitted with the Merlin 61 engine with a two-stage supercharger. Low down these highly supercharged engines became a liability, for although the big superchargers absorbed power, this could not be used to full effect, resulting in the fighter's range and endurance suffering accordingly.

The solution was to produce a fighter optimised for low altitude operations, which was fitted with the 'M' suffix Merlin engine with the supercharger blower cropped to 9.5-in diameter. The Merlin 45M, the 50M and the 55M all had a full-throttle height of 6000 ft and delivered up to +18 pounds boost at that altitude.

As a further move to improve the fighter's low altitude performance, the Spitfire's pointed wing tips were removed and streamlined fairings fitted in their place. That reduced the wing span to 32 ft 6 ins and the wing area by 11 square feet, which gave worthwhile improvements in

BR202 served as test aircraft for the trials of the 170-gal ferry tank, conducted from Boscombe Down during the summer of 1942 (*via Robertson*)

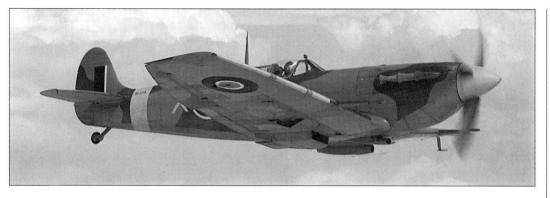

Mk LF VB of No 315 Sqn. The clip wings gave the fighter a clear improvement in diving speed, acceleration and rate of roll. Below 10,000 ft, the maximum speed was increased by about 5 mph, and the only disadvantage was a slight increase in the fighter's minimum turning radius (*via Jarrett*)

Mk LF VB W3834/YO-Q of No 401 'Canadian' Sqn. On the fuselage the aircraft carries the presentation emblem *Corps of Imperial Frontiersmen*. Delivered new to No 266 Sqn in September 1941, it subsequently served with Nos 154, 421 and 416 Sqns before reaching No 401 in June 1943. It was passed to No 126 Sqn, before being assigned to second line tasks (*RCAF*)

performance. Compared with the Mk V with standard-span wings, the clipped-wing fighter dived faster, had better acceleration and a faster rate of roll. Below 10,000 ft its maximum speed was also roughly 5 mph greater. Low down the only disadvantage of the clipped wings was that they gave a slight increase in the fighter's minimum turning radius. The combination of the low-altitude-rated Merlin and clipped wings made the Spitfire LF V a handy fighter at low altitude, with a maximum speed of $338\frac{1}{2}$ mph at 2000 ft and $355\frac{1}{2}$ mph at 5900 ft.

Many of the aircraft converted into LF Vs were Mk VBs taken from storage, some of which bore the scars of earlier actions and hard usage. Compared with other fighter types in service, they were regarded as 'clapped out', which promptly resulted in the LF V being nicknamed 'the clipped, cropped and clapped Spitty', referring to its wings, supercharger and age respectively!

Despite the unkind epithet, there can be no doubt that these modifications added more than two years to the Spitfire V's life as an effective air superiority fighter, for as late as August 1944, the Air Defence of Great Britain organisation retained eleven LF V squadrons in its front-line strength. In its domain below 6000 ft, this version was as fast in level flight as the Fw 190 and faster than the Bf 109G. Provided it had top cover from fighters with a better high altitude performance, the LF V could give any opposing type a hard tussle low down.

ACTION OVER NORTH-WEST EUROPE

By June 1941 six RAF fighter squadrons had converted Spitfire Vs, or were in the process of doing so. That month saw Germany launch a massive attack on the Soviet Union. Eager to support his new ally, Prime Minister Winston Churchill assured the Soviet government that he would do all he could to hold down German forces in the west. This fundamental change in the course of the war put the RAF under strong political pressure to adopt an even more aggressive stance over occupied Europe, and the so-called 'Circus' operations came to form an important aspect of the new offensive posture.

The 'Circus' was a daylight attack performed by a small force of bombers – perhaps as few as six aircraft – escorted by more than a dozen squadrons of fighters. The primary object of these operations was to draw German fighters into the air, and thus allow British fighters to bring them into action and inflict casualties. The destruction of targets was a matter of secondary importance.

Typical of these operations was Circus No 62, staged on 7 August 1941. Six Blenheims were to attack the power station at Lille, covered by no fewer than eighteen squadrons of Spitfires and two of Hurricanes. Six of the units – Nos 72, 92, 603, 609, 611 and 616 Sqns – operated Spitfire Vs, whilst a further four units – Nos 41, 403, 485 and 610 Sqns – were in

Pilots of No 609 Squadron in an impromptu game of cricket at their dispersal at Biggin Hill in the summer of 1941. The Mk VB providing the backdrop is W3238/PR-B *The London Butcher*, the personal mount of the unit commander, Sqn Ldr `Mickey' Robinson. Robinson amassed several victories while flying this machine, notably on 3 July 1941 when he received credit for two Bf 109Fs destroyed and one damaged. He was killed in action in April 1942 when his victory score stood at 16 destroyed, 4 and 1 shared probably destroyed and 8 and 1 shared damaged. The wicket keeper is 'ace-to-be' Sgt Tommy Rigler, who would amass a victory score of 8 destroyed, 1 probably destroyed and 2 and 1shared damaged, all during a one-year period while flying with No 609 Sqn (*via Jerry Scutts*)

Wg Cdr Douglas Bader, commander of the Tangmere Wing, climbs out of his personal Mk VA, W3185/D-B *Lord Lloyd 1*. He was flying this aircraft on 9 August 1941 when he was shot down and taken prisoner. At the time of his capture his victory score was 20 and 4 shared destroyed, 6 and 1 shared probably destroyed and 11 damaged (*via Sarkar*)

the process of re-equipping with the new variant, and thus flew both it and their older Mk IIs. The remaining six units equipped with the earlier Spitfire variant – Nos 71, 111, 222, 452, 485 and 602 Sqns – flew close escort and escort cover for the bombers. The top cover force comprised three Mk V units from the Biggin Hill Wing – Nos 72, 92 and 609 Sqns. The Target Support Force comprised the Hornchurch Wing – Nos 403, 603 and 611 Sqns

Bader is seen here flanked (to his right) by two of those who flew in his flight when he led the Tangmere Wing, namely Flg Off 'Johnnie' Johnson and Flt Lt 'Cocky' Dundas. The former went on to become the greatest exponent of the Spitfire in action, ending the war credited with 34 and 7 shared enemy aircraft destroyed, 3 and 2 shared probably destroyed and 10 and 3 shared damaged. 'Cocky' Dundas finished with 4 and 6 shared destroyed, 2 shared probably destroyed and 1 shared damaged

Sqn Ldr Christopher 'Bunny' Currant commanded No 501 Sqn from August 1941 until June 1942. At the end of the war his victory score was 10 and 5 shared destroyed, 2 probably destroyed and 12 damaged (*via Sarkar*)

– and the Tangmere Wing – Nos 41, 610 and 616 Sqns – wholly or partially equipped with Mk Vs.

Only a few German fighters came up to harry the main raiding force, and the after-action report from the Tangmere Wing, led by Wg Cdr Douglas Bader, described the scrappy combats that followed;

'Wing met over base, crossed the English coast over Hastings at 23/24/25000 feet and made landfall over Le Touquet at 23/24/27,000 ft. A large orbit was made between Merville and Le Touquet. Proceeded towards the target area, encountering many Me 109s approximately 1000 ft above. Enemy aircraft came down out of the sun on the starboard quarter – the Wing turned to attack and the enemy aircraft dived away refusing to engage, but dogfights ensued. These tactics ensued over the Hazebrouck, Merville and Lille areas and on the way back to the French coast where the 109s broke away. The coast was recrossed by squadrons separately between Le Touquet and Boulogne; all the pilots and aircraft had returned by 18.55, with the exception of one from No 41 Sqn (Flt Lt Gilbert Draper was shot down and captured, Ed.).'

At the same time, the Biggin Hill and Hornchurch Wings fought similarly inconclusive engagements. The Blenheim force reached Lille unscathed, only to find its target shrouded in cloud. It turned away and released its bombs on the alternative target, which consisted of barges in the canal at Gravelines. The German fighters concentrated their main effort against the two squadrons of Hurricanes and three of Spitfire IIs

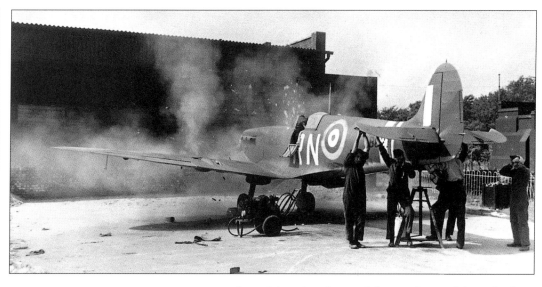

Mk VB of No 72 Sqn spews fourth rounds from its 20 mm Hispano cannon during firing at the stop butts, probably at Biggin Hill, in September 1941. Note the hefty brass cartridge cases falling under the port wing. Almost certainly this firing was set up for the camera-man, for it formed no part of the gun harmonization process for the Spitfire. If the serviceability of a gun was suspect, that weapon was usually removed and tested individually (*via Sarkar*)

covering the withdrawal, and in total the RAF lost six fighters for three enemy machines claimed destroyed and three probably destroyed.

Circus No 62 illustrates well the difficulties involved for Fighter Command in performing these missions. The German fighter force could choose when, where and whether to engage the raiding force, and when it did engage, it invariably did so on terms that gave its fighters the best possible chance to inflict losses at the lowest possible cost.

Expressed merely in terms of aircraft destroyed on each side, the 'Circus' operations were not, and were unlikely ever to be, a success for the RAF. Yet the political imperative dictated that German day fighter units be held back in the west, and the 'Circus' was the RAF's chosen instrument for doing so. There was a further consideration. In war a fighter force needs opportunities to fight or its morale, its fighting spirit and its fighting capability, will wither away. By sending units on frequent offensive operations over enemy territory, Sir Sholto Douglas ensured that Fighter Command remained an effective force during the difficult years of 1941/42.

An armourer of No 72 Sqn is seen cleaning the barrel of the port Hispano cannon

ENTER THE FW 190

As observed earlier, when it entered service the Spitfire VB was broadly comparable in performance with its best German counterpart, the Bf 109F. That situation would not last for much longer, however, for in the late summer of 1941 the Luftwaffe introduced a new, and potentially more effective, fighter into service – the Focke-Wulf Fw 190 (see Osprey volume *Aircraft of the Aces 9 Focke-Wulf Fw 190 Aces of the Western Front* for further details).

When the new German fighter first appeared in action over northern France it came as a severe shock to Fighter Command. The Fw 190 was 25-30 mph faster than the Spitfire V at most altitudes, and it out-climbed, out-dived and out-rolled the British fighter. Indeed, the Spitfire V's only advantage over its new opponent was that it could turn tighter (for a comparative assessment of the two fighters see the Appendix).

Fortunately for the RAF the new fighter suffered teething problems which saw the aircraft's BMW radial engine often overheat in flight to the point where the pilot often had to shut down or risk a fire. Indeed, things got so bad that for a time Fw 190 pilots were forbidden to fly over the sea beyond gliding range from the coast. Moreover, with bulk of the Luftwaffe now committed on the eastern front, the fighter force remaining in the west was relatively small.

Low altitude beat-up of the No 72 Sqn dispersal at Biggin Hill by one of the unit Mk VBs

Flaps down on the landing approach for Northolt, a Mk VB of No 308 'Polish' Sqn returns to base (*via Sarkar*)

As the weather deteriorated during the latter part of 1941, the RAF flew progressively fewer 'Circus' and other offensive operations over Occupied Europe – there were five such missions flown in October, two in November and none at all in December.

During 1941 Spitfire production far exceeded losses, allowing a massive expansion in the number of units operating the type. In the Battle of Britain only 19 squadrons had operated Spitfires, but by September 1941 there were 27. And by the end of 1941 Fighter Command had 46 squadrons of Spitfires, most of them flying Mk Vs.

BLACK SPITFIRES

In November 1941 No 111 Sqn moved the short distance from North Weald to Debden with its Spitfire VBs and, along with the similarly-equipped No 65 Sqn, began flying a programme of night training exercises. This unusual turn of events was prompted by Fighter Command fears that the Luftwaffe might resume its large-scale night bombing offensive on Britain, and in order to counter this threat, a high-speed night interception force was required.

For the new role the two units' Spitfires were repainted in matt black overall, and although the national markings and squadron codes were retained on the fuselage and fin, those above and below the wings being painted over. Groundcrews fitted 'fishtail' exhausts in place of the previous circular type, plus 'blinker' strips just forward of the cockpit – both modifications went some way to reducing the effects of exhaust glare on pilots' nocturnal vision during night sorties.

The Spitfires were to work with radar-laid searchlights, employing so-called 'Smack' interception tactics. When enemy aircraft approached the coast, the sector controller ordered the fighters to scramble and the Spitfire pilots would duly take-off individually and head for their pre-briefed patrol area marked by a single vertical searchlight beam. Once in the patrol area the pilot would fly orbits around the beam at the briefed altitude, and wait. When an enemy aircraft neared the area the searchlight

Flt Lt Howard-Williams of No 118 Sqn is seen soon after his return from a fierce combat over northern France on 2 February 1942 in which he claimed a Bf 109F destroyed and two damaged. During the action his own aircraft collected a cannon shell hit. At the end of the war his victory score was 4 and 1 shared destroyed, 1 probably destroyed and 2 damaged (*via Sarkar*)

Mk VB AD199 served with Nos 71, 145 and 308 Sqns before it reached No 403 'Canadian' Sqn in March 1942. A couple of weeks after its arrival the Spitfire suffered serious damage in this altercation with a ground defence pillbox at Hornchurch. After repair, the aircraft served with Nos 121 and 277 Sqns – whilst serving with the latter unit it flew air sea rescue operations at the time of the Normandy invasion in June 1944. The Spitfire survived the war and was struck off charge in October 1945

beam wavered, then depressed to 20°, pointing in the direction the fighter was required to fly. Sgt Peter Durnford, who would gain ace status flying day fighter missions later in the war, explained the rest of the procedure;

'We would fly along the beam until another searchlight came on, pointing up vertically. Then it would waggle and point in the next direction we were to go. When we got close to the intruder we were to get the radio call "Cone!", and several searchlights would switch on and cone the target with their beams. Once we had the target in sight we were to engage it.'

The two squadrons regularly practised the 'Smack' procedures, but for some reason they were not allowed to test them against friendly aircraft. This meant that the first time the pilots used the procedure 'for real' would be against an enemy. In the event the expected air attacks failed to materialise, and black Spitfires never went into action at night, although they would do so on one occasion by day.

On 12 February 1942 the battle cruisers *Scharnhorst* and *Gneisenau*, the cruiser *Prinz Eugen* and several smaller warships dashed north-eastward through the Strait of Dover on their way back to Germany from various French ports. Every available Luftwaffe fighter in the west took part in the covering operation. Durnford recalled;

'We had been on readiness during the night, sleeping in the dispersal hut. There was some local flying in the morning, then we knocked off. Suddenly we were called back to readiness. The Wing Commander Flying dashed into the briefing room and said "The German fleet is coming through the Channel, follow me!"

'He took off and we followed him. We were supposed to rendezvous with the Spitfire squadrons from North Weald, but the weather was terrible and we missed them. We went out over the sea, and the next thing I knew we had run into a whole lot of '109s. There was a terrific low level scrap and our squadron was split up. I fired on a '109 and saw strikes around the cockpit – it rolled on its back and went down. Due to the very

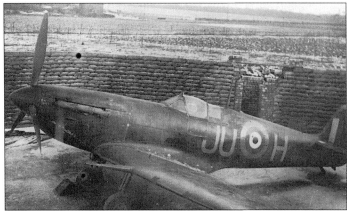

Top, middle and bottom
Sgt Peter Durnford of No 111 Sqn is seen at Debden with Mk VB JU-H in December 1941. The unit was assigned to night interception duties in co-operation with searchlights for a period of about two months. During this time the aircraft were painted in matt black overall, with the serial number and wing roundels painted over (*Durnford*)

Mk VB YQ-A was flown by Sqn Ldr Colin Gray whilst OC No 616 Sqn, based at King's Cliff, in January 1942. New Zealander Gray's career flying Spitfires in combat is described in the two earlier works in this series, *Late Mark Spitfire Aces 1942-45* and *Spitfire Mark I/II Aces 1939-41*. His command of No 616 Sqn with Spitfire VBs lasted from September 1941 to February 1942. At that time the unit was based in the Midlands, which presented Gray with few opportunities to engage enemy aircraft – he achieved no victories during this period. At the end of the war his total score, gained mainly on Mk Is and IXs, stood at 27 and 2 shared destroyed, 6 and 4 shared probably destroyed and 12 damaged (*Thomas*)

low height, 100 ft or so, it must have gone in (I was later awarded a "Probable").

'Then I passed over some ships which threw a lot of flak at me and my No 2. We got separated and in the end I decided to go home as I was getting short of fuel. Visibility was poor and I had a job finding somewhere to land. In the end I put down at North Weald and just as I landed the prop stopped. I had run out of fuel after 2 hours 10 minutes airborne.'

This was Peter Durnford's sole encounter with the enemy while flying a black Spitfire. After that incident the two squadrons were released from night operations, and the following month their Spitfires were repainted in normal day-fighter colours. Durnford later achieved ace status whilst flying Spitfire VIs with No 124 Sqn over the invasion beaches of Dieppe in August 1942, attaining a final score of five aircraft shot down and one damaged.

HARD TIMES

During the spring of 1942 the steady improvement in the weather allowed the RAF to resume its daylight offensive against targets in Occupied Europe. Despite its limitations, the Spitfire V remained the most effective fighter available, and it was therefore made to bear the brunt of the air-to-air fighting. In a move to improve the overall effectiveness of the force, six squadrons in the Hornchurch and Kenley Wings (initially Nos 64, 313, 402, 457, 485 and 602 Sqns) received Spitfire VBs modified to carry the new 30-gallon drop tank. The additional fuel allowed these units to fly at higher throttle settings for longer periods, and thus cruise at greater altitudes. These units provided top cover for the other squadrons taking part in the attacks, and although the improvements to the Spitfire's speed and altitude were not large, RAF pilots pitted against an ever-increasing number of Fw 190s needed all the help they could get.

Meanwhile, on the Luftwaffe side, all six *Gruppen* of *Jagdgeschwader* 2 and 26 had re-equipped with the Fw 190, and between them could now

German troops pose with Mk VB RS-T after Wg Cdr Robert Stanford Tuck, OC Biggin Hill Wing, crash landed in France on 28 February 1942 after his aircraft was hit by flak. Although the Spitfire's serial number was painted over, it is believed to be BL336. At the time of his capture Tuck was credited with 27 and 2 shared destroyed, 6 probably destroyed and 6 and 1 shared damaged

Heavily posed line-up of Mk VCs, with pilots in the cockpits and 'busy' groundcrews, belonging to No 91 Sqn at Hawkinge in May 1942. The aircraft on the far right is AB216/DL-Z *Nigeria Oyo Province*, which was flown by the commander, Sqn Ldr Bob Oxspring – he is seen here strapping in. A Battle of Britain veteran, Oxspring survived the war with a victory total of 13 and 1 shared destroyed, 2 probably destroyed and 13 damaged (*via Robertson*)

Mk VB SH-Z *Atchashikar*, flown by Sqn Ldr Wilfred Duncan-Smith (OC No 64 Sqn), is seen in May 1942. Although the aircraft's serial was painted over it is thought to be BM476, delivered new to the unit the month prior to this photo being taken. Duncan-Smith was flying the aircraft on 17 May when he was credited with the destruction of an Fw 190. The Spitfire went on to serve with Nos 154, 165, 122, 234, 303, 26 Sqns and No 58 OTU, before it was written off in a flying accident in May 1943. At the end of the war Duncan-Smith's victory score was 17 and 2 shared destroyed, 6 and 2 shared probably destroyed and 8 damaged (*via Robertson*)

Mk VB BL584/DW-X of No 610 Sqn, seen at Ludham in July 1942, was flown by Flt Lt Denis Crowley-Milling. At the end of the war Crowley-Milling's victory score was 4 and 1 shared destroyed, 2 probably destroyed and 1 and 1 shared damaged (*via Sarkar*)

muster about 260 of these formidable fighters. The engine troubles that had initially plagued the fighter were by now largely cured, allowing German pilots to exploit their mounts' capabilities to the full, and thus engage with greater confidence.

Matters finally came to a head on 1 June 1942 during Circus No 178. The attacking force comprised eight bomb-carrying Hurricanes attacking a target in northern Belgium. Seven squadrons of Spitfire Vs from the Hornchurch and Biggin Hill Wings escorted the force, and four squadrons from the Debden Wing provided support over the target area. Positioned by radar and led by fighter ace Hauptmann 'Pips' Priller, some 40 Fw 190s of I. and III./JG 26 'bounced' the raiding force from out of

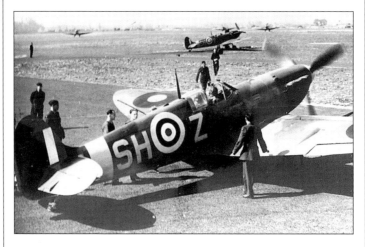

25

Groundcrewmen work on a Mk VB of No 332 'Norwegian' Sqn. On top of the 'trolley acc' starter unit plugged into the aircraft is a 'Chore Horse' motor to re-charge the accumulators (*via Jarrett*)

the sun. The Debden Wing took the force of the attack and lost eight Spitfires, including that flown by its commander – a further five Spitfires returned with battle damage. No Focke-Wulf suffered serious damage during the encounter.

The following day proved equally disastrous for a Fighter Command unit. Two wings of Spitfires flew through the St Omer area on a 'Rodeo' operation, a large-scale fighter sweep with no bombers. Usually the Luftwaffe ignored such incursions, but not on this occasion. Fw 190s of I. and II./JG 26 delivered a massed attack, and No 403 (Canadian) Sqn, led the redoubtable Battle of Britain ace, Sqn Ldr Alan Deere, was on the receiving end. The following description of the combat was published in his autobiography, *Nine Lives* (Hodder & Stoughton 1959);

'Shortly after we crossed the French coast (as top sqaudron in the North

Sqn Ldr Michael Pedley was OC No 131 Sqn between November 1941 and August 1942. At the end of the war his victory score was 3 and 2 shared destroyed and 3 damaged. No 131 Sqn were adopted by the people of Kent soon after the unit's formation in 1941, and its aircraft were duly decorated with the prancing white horse emblem of the county – suitably modified through the addition of wings. This Spitfire, *Spirit of Kent/Lord Cornwallis*, was just one of a number of machines paid for by individuals or organisations and presented to the RAF (*via Robertson*)

Weald Wing, flying above the Hornchurch Wing, Ed.) on the way in, the Controller reported enemy activity to the raid. Varied reports on the strength of the reaction were passed over the R/T, but there was no sign of enemy fighters until about 20 miles from Le Touquet on the way out. At this point, "Mitzi" (Flt Lt Edward V Darling, a five-kill Battle of Britain ace who was serving as a flight commander with No 403 Sqn, and who was subsequently shot down and killed on this mission) reported a formation of about a dozen Fw 190s directly behind, at the same height and closing fast. I picked them up immediately and warned the rest of the squadron to prepare for a "break". We had practised a manoeuvre to cope with just this sort of contingency; one section would break upwards in the opposite direction from the other two which would turn into the attacking fighters.

'"They're getting close, Toby Leader", a breathless and worried "Mitzi" urged some action.

'"OK Blue One, I see them. Wait for the order to break".

'When I judged that the Huns were about the right distance away to suit the manoeuvre I intended to carry out, I gave the order.

'"Toby squadron, break left".

'On my right, Yellow section broke upwards and away while, with Blue section outside me, I turned hard into the closing enemy fighters. About half-way around the break I looked for Yellow section above and to my left and was startled to see another formation of Fw 190s emerging through a thin layer of stratus cloud about 2000 ft above and on our beam. It was too late to do anything

about it; the first formation of Fw 190s was head on to my section, which had now almost completed its turn, and there was only time for a split-second burst as the Huns pulled up and above us.

'"Watch out, Red Leader, more of them coming down from above and to our right".

'Savagely I hauled my reluctant Spitfire around to meet this new attack and, the next moment I was engulfed in enemy fighters – above, below and on both sides, they

Sqn Ldr Reginald Grant was OC No 485 'New Zealand' Sqn between May 1942 and March 1943. A Kiwi himself, Grant was killed flying a Mustang III in February 1944 whilst leading No 122 Wing on a Ramrod over France. At the time of his death his victory score stood at 7 and 1 shared destroyed and 1 probably destroyed (*via Franks*)

Western Australian-born Sqn Ldr Hugo 'Sinker' Armstrong (right) had served as a flight commander with the Spitfire Mk VB-equipped No 72 Sqn in the spring and summer of 1942 before being given command of No 611 Sqn at Biggin Hill in September of that year. He was killed in action over the Channel on 3 February 1943 flying a Mk IX, and at the time of his death his victory score stood at 10 and 1 shared destroyed, 3 probably destroyed and 2 damaged. To Armstrong's right is Sqn Ldr J H 'Garth' Slater, who was lost in action on 14 March 1943 whilst flying as a supernumery squadron leader attached to No 611 Sqn (*via Franks*)

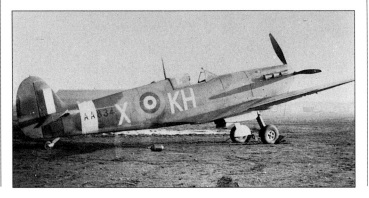

Mk VB AA834 was on strength with No 403 Sqn at the time the unit was badly mauled by the Fw 190s of JG 26 on 2 June 1942. It survived with the Canadian unit until lost in action on 27 April 1943 whilst flying from Kenley (*Bracken via Fochuk*)

Sqn Ldr Jan Zumbach was OC No 303 'Polish' Sqn from May to December 1942. When the war ended his victory score stood at 12 and 2 shared destroyed, 5 probably destroyed and 1 damaged (*B Arct Collection via Matusiak*)

crowded in on my section. Ahead and above. I caught a glimpse of a Fw 190 as it poured cannon shells into the belly of an unsuspecting Spitfire. For a brief second the Spitfire seemed to stop in mid-air, and the next instant it folded inwards and broke in two, the pieces plummeting earthwards; a terrifying demonstration of the Fw 190's four cannon and two machine guns.

'I twisted and turned my aircraft in an endeavour to avoid being jumped and at the same time to get myself in a favourable position for attack. Never had I seen the Hun stay and fight it out as these Focke-Wulf pilots were doing. In Messerschmitt 109s the Hun tactics had always followed the same pattern – a quick pass and away, sound tactics against Spitfires with their superior turning circle. Not so these Fw 190 pilots. They were full of confidence.

'There was no lack of targets (30+ Fw 190A-2s and A-3s, Ed.), but precious few Spitfires (just 12) to take them on. I could see my number two, Sgt Murphy, still hanging grimly on to my tail but it was impossible to tell how many Spitfires were in the area, or how many had survived the unexpected onslaught which had developed from both sides as the squadron turned to meet the threat from the rear. Break followed attack, attack followed break, and all the time the determined Murphy hung to my tail until finally, when I was just about short of ammunition and pumping what was left at a Fw 190, I heard him call.

'"Break right, Red One; I'll get him".

'As I broke, I saw Murphy pull up after a Fw 190 as it veered away from me, thwarted in its attack by his prompt action. My ammunition expended, I sought a means of retreat from a sky still generously sprinkled with hostile enemy fighters, but no Spitfires that I could see. In a series of turns and dives I made my way out until I was clear of the coast, and diving full throttle I headed for home.'

During the desperate seven-minute brawl between I. and II./JG 26 and No 403 Sqn, seven of the latter had been shot down – none of the Fw 190s had suffered any serious hits. Two more Spitfires struggled back across the Channel with chronic battle damage, and one of these was latter classified a write-off.

This photo of Zumbach in the cockpit of Mk VB EN951/RF-D shows his 'Angry Duck' emblem and victory scoreboard as they appeared in October 1942. Delivered new to No 133 Sqn in June 1942, this aircraft was turned over to No 303 Sqn shortly afterwards, where it soon became Zumbach's personnel mount. He flew this Mk VB until he relinquished command of the squadron in December 1942. It later served with Nos 315, 504 and 129 Sqns, before going to the Central Gunnery School. By war's end it was still being used as an instructional airframe

This Mk VB of No 302 Sqn wears the four white nose stripes as employed by many Spitfire units tasked with supporting the Dieppe landing on 19 August 1942. This aircraft was flown on that day by Wg Cdr Stefan Witorzenc, who was then commanding the 1st Polish Fighter Wing

A few weeks later the C-in-C Fighter Command, Air Chief Marshal Sir Sholto Douglas, wrote a strongly worded letter to the Under Secretary of State for Air, Lord Sherwood, in which he complained that his force had lost the technical edge it had had over the Luftwaffe. He went on;

'There is . . . no doubt in my mind, nor in the minds of my fighter pilots, that the Fw 190 is the best all-round fighter in the world today.'

Relief would soon be at hand, however, in the shape of the new Spitfire Mk IX. Like the Mk V, this aircraft was a hasty conversion of an available airframe to take a new engine giving greater power. In this case the airframe was that of the Mk VC, and the engine was the Merlin 61 with a two-stage supercharger (see Osprey volume *Aircraft of the Aces 5 Late Mark Spitfire Aces 1942-45* for more details). The first squadron of Mk IXs – No 64 – was already forming and the new variant went into action at the end of July. With a performance closely comparable with that of the Fw 190, the Mk IX would be used initially to provide top cover for units flying Mk Vs. By August 1942, Fighter Command had four squadrons operational with the new variant, and other units were in the process of forming.

OPERATION *JUBILEE*

Spitfire V units had their hardest day's fighting ever on 19 August 1942 in support of Operation *Jubilee*, the amphibious landing at the port of Dieppe in northern France. A total of 48 Spitfire squadrons were involved, 42 with Mk Vs, 2 with Mk VIs and 4 with Mk IXs.

Battle of Britain ace Sqn Ldr Peter Brothers led the Mk Vs of No 602 Sqn into action in four patrols that day, and claimed one Fw 190 damaged. He recalled the sharp differences in the nature of the air fighting as the day progressed;

'Operation *Jubilee* itself was interesting in terms of the way it showed how a battle develops. My squadron was one of the first on patrol over the beaches at first light at 2000 ft, and at that point there was virtually no (air) activity at all. We were duly relieved and went back to refuel, and when we returned for our second sweep activity had well and truly started, with the (German) medium bomber formations trying to get up to the cloud base at 4000 ft for protection. As the weather improved we increased our patrolling ceiling to 5000 ft, and by the end of our fourth, and last, sortie in the late afternoon, we were cruising at 20,000 ft! This day perfectly illustrated how crucial the advantage of height is in aerial warfare, and as the weather improved, we took advantage of it accordingly.

'Of the four sweeps we flew that day, the second patrol was the most exciting from our squadron's point of view as we intercepted a large formation of Ju 88s and Do 217s, escorted by a fair number of Fw 190s. I made passes at both types of German bomber, but on every occasion had to break off my attacks due to the overwhelming number of Fw 190s in the area – indeed, my number two, Plt Off M F Goodchap, was shot down and captured. Such was the ferocity of the battle, it was impossible to concentrate on downing a single machine, and I had to resort to taking pot shots at enemy aircraft as they passed through my field of fire during my hour-long series of evasive manoeuvres.'

Wg Cdr Stefan Witorzenc flew in the Battle of Britain and went on to become one of the most eminent Polish fighter leaders. At the end of the war his victory score stood at 5 and 1 shared destroyed and 2 damaged (*Flt Lt Bochmiak via Matusiak*)

Mk VBs of No 310 'Czech' Sqn are seen here wearing the Dieppe operation markings. During *Jubilee* the unit flew from Redhill under the command of Sqn Ldr Frantisek Dolezal, who was credited with a Do 217 probably destroyed and an Fw 190 damaged over the invasion beach (*via Hurt*)

The Mk V units flew more than 150 squadron-sized patrols and 1800 sorties (out of just over 2600 undertaken by Allied aircraft that day) on the 19th, suffering their heaviest single day's casualties ever – 53 aircraft downed out of a total Allied loss of 100.

LOW ALTITUDE OPERATIONS

During the year following the introduction of the Spitfire IX in July 1942, several UK squadrons re-equipped with the new variant, yet during the summer of 1943 Mk Vs still dominated Fighter Command's order of battle. By then the 'Circus' operation was a thing of the past, having been replaced by the 'Ramrod' – an attack by a large force of bombers or fighter-bombers tasked with the sole purpose of destroying targets. In this type of operation the primary role of the escorting fighters was to protect the bombers from fighter attack, and during Ramrod S.36, flown on 6 September 1943, of the 32 Spitfire squadrons that took part no fewer than 18 were still flying Mk Vs.

Although it was outclassed at high altitude, with modifications the Mk V remained a formidable opponent low down. The Spitfire LF V, optimised for the low altitude air superiority role, was fitted with an 'M' series engine equipped with a cropped supercharger impeller (see Chapter Two). At altitudes below 6000 ft this version was as fast as the Fw 190, and faster than a Bf 109G.

As late as June 1944 No 11 Group retained a few frontline fighter units wholly or partially equipped with the Spitfire LF V. Among these were Nos 234, 345, 350 and 501 Sqns, all of which flew combat patrols over France during the Normandy invasion and the weeks that followed.

On 8 June 1944, during an engagement near Le Havre, American pilot Flt Lt David 'Foob' Fairbanks (who later 'made ace' on Tempests) of No 501 Sqn was flying LF VB X4272 when he shot down a Bf 109 and damaged another. This particular airframe had had a remarkable history, having performed its maiden flight as a Mk I as long ago as August 1940. Before delivery to a squadron it was modified to carry an armament of two 20 mm cannon and four machine guns, thus becoming a Mk IB. At the end of 1940 it went to No 92 Sqn and saw action, being credited with at least one victory. Early in 1941 the aircraft was one of those sent to Rolls-

Wg Cdr Minden Blake was OC Portreath Wing in the summer of 1942. During the Dieppe landings he was credited with the destruction of an Fw 190, but shortly afterwards Blake was himself shot down and taken prisoner. At the time of his capture his victory score was 10 and 3 shared destroyed and 1 shared damaged (*via Franks*)

Minden Blake was flying Mk VB W3561/M-B when he was shot down and captured whilst supporting the Dieppe invasion on 19 August 1942. At that time it is likely that the aircraft was carrying the Operation *Jubilee* stripes round the engine cowling (*via Franks*)

Royce for installation of a Merlin 45 engine, and in March it was returned
to No 92 Sqn as part of the initial batch of Mk VBs. Later it served for a
time with No 222 Sqn, before being placed in storage. X4272 was then
selected for conversion to LF Mk VB standard, and the fighter was still
flying with No 501 Sqn in July 1944 when the unit finally re-equipped
with Tempests.

In the course of their numerous incursions into Occupied Europe
between 1941 and 1943, UK-based Spitfire V units had sometimes suffered a 'bloody nose' at the hands of the German defenders. Yet in mount-
ing the 'Circus', 'Rodeo' and 'Ramrod' operations, the raiders invariably
possessed two important advantages. Firstly, the RAF held the strategic
initiative, which essentially meant that if the attacks became too costly
they could slow the pace of operations, and perhaps shift to easier targets
closer to the coast. And secondly, the RAF fighter units enjoyed a clear
numerical superiority over their opponents. Some 1200+ miles away in
the Mediterranean, the Spitfire V squadrons operating from Malta in
1942 faced a quite different type of battle. They were pitched into a life-
or-death struggle against a numerically superior foe bent on their destruction. This aspect of the Spitfire V story is described in the next chapter.

Mk VBs of Nos 416 and 421 'Canadian' Sqns with the white nose strip applied to 'Eastland' aircraft taking part in Exercise *Spartan* in March 1943. This large-scale exercise was staged to test procedures for tactical deployment and field operations in preparation for the invasion of France the following year (*RCAF*)

Canadians Sqn Ldr Geoff Northcott (seated) and Wg Cdr Lloyd Chadburn pose for the camera at Digby in the summer of 1943 alongside the former's LF VB EP120, which carries his kill tally. Northcott was OC No 402 Sqn at the time, whilst Chadburn was Wing Leader of the Canadian squadrons at Digby. The latter had scored 5 and 3 shared destroyed, 5 and 1 shared probably destroyed and 7 and 2 shared damaged by the time he was killed in a collision with another Spitfire over the Normandy beaches on 13 June 1944 (*via Fochuk*)

1
Mk VA W3185/D-B *Lord Lloyd I* of Wg Cdr Douglas Bader, OC Tangmere Wing, Tangmere, August 1941

2
Mk VB RS-T of Wg Cdr Robert Stanford Tuck, OC Biggin Hill Wing, Biggin Hill, February 1942

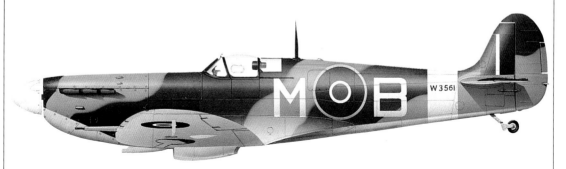

3
Mk VB W3561/M-B of Wg Cdr Minden Blake, OC Portreath Wing, Portreath, summer 1942

4
Mk VB AB502/IR-G of Wg Cdr Ian Gleed, OC No 244 Wing, Goubrine South, 16 April 1943

5
Mk VC BR498/PP-H of Wg Cdr Peter Prosser Hanks, OC of the Luqa Wing, Luqa, October 1942

6
Mk VC BS234 (A58-95)/CRC of Wg Cdr Clive Caldwell, OC No 1 Fighter Wing, RAAF, Livingstone, March 1943

7
Mk VC BS164 (A58-63)/DL-K of Sqn Ldr Eric Gibbs, OC No 54 Sqn, Darwin, July 1943

8
Mk VB SH-Z *Atchashikar* of Sqn Ldr Wilfred Duncan-Smith, OC No 64 Sqn, Hornchurch, May 1942

9
Mk VB BM361/XR-C of Sqn Ldr Chesley Peterson, OC No 71 'Eagle' Sqn, Gravesend, August 1942

10
Mk VC AB216/DL-Z *Nigeria Oyo Province* of Sqn Ldr Robert Oxspring, OC No 91 Sqn, Hawkinge, May 1942

11
Mk VB R6923/QJ-S of Flg Off Alan Wright, No 92 Sqn, Biggin Hill, May 1941

12
Mk VB W3312/QJ-J *Moonraker* of Sqn Ldr James Rankin, OC No 92 Sqn, Biggin Hill, August 1941

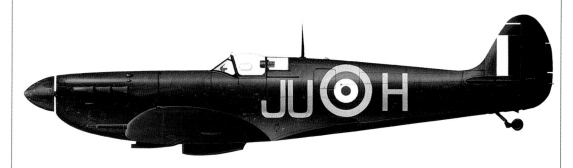

13
Mk VB JU-H of Sgt Peter Durnford, No 111 Sqn, Debden, December 1941

14
Mk VB BP850/F of Flt Sgt Patrick Schade, No 126 Sqn, Takali, April 1942

15
Mk VC BR112/X of Sgt Claude Weaver of No 185 Sqn, Krendi, September 1942

16
Mk VB AD233/ZD-F *West Borneo I* of Sqn Ldr Richard Milne, OC No 222 Sqn, North Weald, March 1942

17
Mk VC JK715/SN-A of Sqn Ldr Evan Mackie, OC No 243 Sqn, Hal Far, June 1943

18
Mk VB AB262/GN-B of Flg Off Robert McNair, No 249 Sqn, Takali, March 1942

19
Mk VC BR323/S of Sgt George Beurling, No 249 Sqn, Takali, July 1942

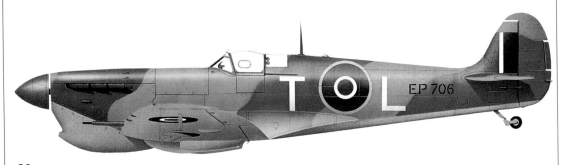

20
Mk VB EP706/T-L of Sqn Ldr Maurice Stephens, No 249 Sqn, Takali, October 1942

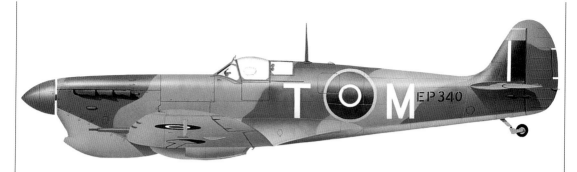

21
Mk VB EP340/T-M of Flg Off John McElroy, No 249 Sqn, Takali, October 1942

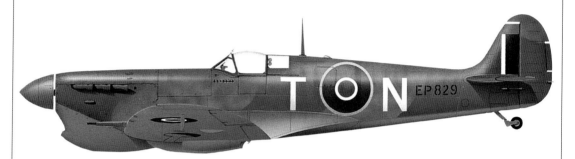

22
Mk VB EP829/T-N of Sqn Ldr Joseph Lynch, OC No 249 Sqn, Krendi, April 1943

23
Mk VB AA853/C-WX (of No 302 'Polish' Sqn) believed flown by Wg Cdr Stefan Witorzenc, OC 1st Polish Fighter Wing, Kirton-in-Lindsey, detached to Heston, Operation *Jubilee*, 19 August 1942

24
Mk VC AB174/RF-Q of Plt Off Antoni Glowacki, No 303 'Polish' Sqn, Kirton-in-Lindsey, August 1942

25
Mk VB BM144/RF-D of Flt Lt Jan Zumbach, No 303 'Polish' Sqn, Northolt, May 1942

26
Mk VB W3718/SZ-S of Flt Lt Stanislaw Skalski, No 316 'Polish' Sqn, Northolt, April 1942

27
Mk VB AA758/JH-V *Bazyli Kuick* of Flt Sgt Stanislaw Brzeski, No 317 'Polish' Sqn, Exeter, November 1941

28
Mk VB EN786/FN-T of Flt Lt Kaj Birksted, No 331 'Norwegian' Sqn, North Weald, June 1942

29
Mk VB BM372/YO-F of Plt Off Donald Morrison, No 401 'Canadian' Sqn, Gravesend, May 1942

30
LF VB EP120/AE-A of Sqn Ldr Geoffrey Northcott, No 402 'Canadian' Sqn, Merston, August 1943

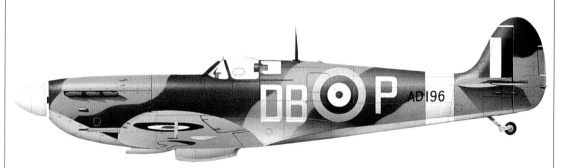

31
Mk AD196/DB-P of Plt Off Henry McLeod, No 411 'Canadian' Sqn, Digby, April 1942

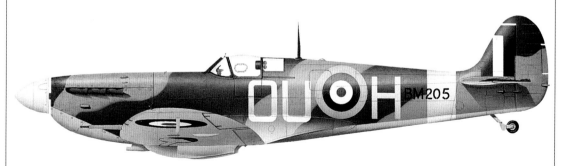

32
Mk VB BM205/OU-H *Nova Scotia* of Plt Off Evan Mackie, No 485 'New Zealand' Sqn, Kenley, April 1942

33
Mk LF VB X4272/SD-J of Flt Lt David Fairbanks, No 501 Sqn, Friston, June 1944

34
Mk VC BP955/J-1 of Flt Lt Denis Barnham, No 601 Sqn, Luqa, April 1942

35
Mk LF VB EP689/UF-X of Sqn Ldr Stanislaw Skalski, OC No 601 Sqn, based at Panchino and Lentini West, July 1943

36
Mk VB W3238/PR-B *The London Butcher* of Sqn Ldr Michael Robinson, OC No 609 Sqn, Biggin Hill, July 1941

37
Mk VB BL584/DW-X of Flt Lt Denis Crowley-Milling of No 610 Sqn, Ludham, July 1942

38
Mk VB (serial overpainted – unknown) YQ-A of Sqn Ldr Colin Gray, OC No 616 Sqn, King's Cliff, January 1942

39
Mk VB EN853/AV-D of Maj William Daley, 335th FS/4th FG, USAAF, Debden, October 1942

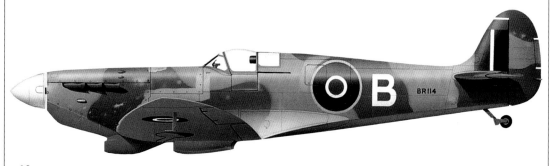

40
Mk VC BR114/B of Flg Off George Genders (and other test pilots), No 103 Maintenance Unit, Aboukir September 1942

1
Sqn Ldr 'Mickey' Robinson, OC No
609 Sqn, Biggin Hill, summer 1941

2
Flg Off 'Gus' Daymond, No 71 'Eagle'
Sqn, North Weald, September 1941

3
Wg Cdr 'Sailor' Malan, OC Biggin Hill
Wing, summer 1941

4
Sgt 'Tommy' Rigler, No 609 Sqn,
Biggin Hill, summer 1941

5
Flt Lt Neville Duke, No 92 Sqn,
Bu Grara, Tunisia, March 1943

6
Wg Cdr Clive Caldwell, OC No 1 Fighter Wing, RAAF, Darwin, May 1943

AIR BATTLE FOR MALTA

I n 1942, the skies over Malta provided both the Spitfire V and its pilots with the most severe test of all, for in that fiery crucible, almost any talented individual who survived long enough in combat would inevitably gain the coveted status of fighter ace.

Lying in the centre of the Mediterranean, the island had huge strategic importance. Bombers, torpedo-bombers and submarines based there

Below and bottom
Spitfire VBs take off from HMS
***Eagle* on the second of the delivery**
runs to Malta, code-named
Operation *Picket I*, on 21 March 1942

Its wing tips removed for ease of handling, this Spitfire is pushed off the deck lift and back into the hangar bay after being loaded aboard USS *Wasp* at Port Glasgow as part of Operation *Calendar*. This photo clearly shows the large blister above each wing synonymous with early Mk VCs, the bulged fairing covering the drum magazines for the two adjacent 20 mm cannon (*USN*)

The flightdeck of *Wasp* at dusk on 19 April 1942. Ranged ready to take-off at first light the following morning are the carrier's own F4F-3 Wildcat fighters which were to provide air cover for the launching operation. Behind them are the Spitfire VCs of No 601 Sqn – the first wave to get airborne. The leading Spitfire was flown by Sqn Ldr 'Jumbo' Gracie, the Battle of Britain ace being the first RAF pilot launched off *Wasp* (*USN*)

took a steady toll of ships carrying supplies and reinforcements for the Axis armies fighting in North Africa, and by the end of 1941 these depredations had reached the point where they could no longer be shrugged off. The Axis high command began detailed planning for a combined airborne and seaborne assault operation to seize Malta.

As an essential preliminary to the invasion, the Luftwaffe transferred more than 400 combat aircraft to airfields in Sicily for the softening-up operations. About half of these were Ju 87 and Ju 88 bombers, with more than 100 Messerschmitt Bf 109Fs also being despatched to provide them

with fighter escort. The bombardment of Malta opened in January 1942, and in a few weeks the air situation for the defenders had reached a critical stage.

The only single-seat fighter type then available for the defence of Malta was the Hurricane II, this obsolescent fighter proving to be no match for the Bf109F it now faced in combat. Losses quickly mounted amongst the defenders. During February airfields and military installations on the island came

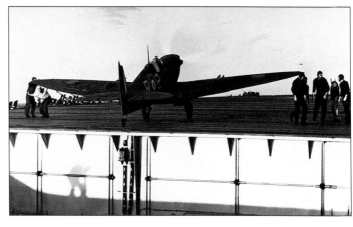

under systematic air attack as some 750 tons of bombs were dropped in just a matter of days. There was little the defenders could do to prevent these devastating raids.

The obvious answer was to move Spitfire squadrons to Malta to defend the island, but how? The strength of the Axis air and naval forces blockading the island ruled out their delivery by freighter, as any such attempt would result in a full scale air-sea battle, with the certainty of heavy losses and little chance of success. Malta is 1100 statute miles from Gibraltar, a distance far beyond the ferry range of the Spitfire at that time. The only feasible method of delivering Spitfires to the island, as was the case with the Hurricanes sent earlier, was to transport them half-way by aircraft carrier. They would then take-off from the deck and fly the rest of the way to the island, but this still left the pilots facing a flight of about 660 miles – a distance about as far as that from London to Prague – to be completed.

As described in Chapter Two, engineers at Supermarine designed a 90-gallon drop tank to provide the necessary extra fuel for the flight. Mk Vs earmarked for delivery to Malta had fittings to carry the new tanks and fuel systems modified to draw fuel from them. The aircraft were also fitted with tropical filters to prevent dust or sand getting into the engine via the carburettor air intake and causing excessive wear during running.

Indicative of the slick take-off timing achieved from *Wasp* during *Calendar*, this No 603 Sqn Spitfire is about to begin its launch run just as the aircraft ahead can be seen as a dot climbing away above the former's starboard wing tip. The lift is already on its way down to pick up the next aircraft, which is in the hangar with its engine running (*USN*)

After taking off from *Wasp* during Operation *Bowery* on 9 May, Plt Off Jerry Smith found that his ferry tank would not deliver fuel. After waiting for the rest of the Spitfires to get airborne, the Canadian pilot landed his fighter back on the carrier's deck – he was guided aboard by future ranking US Navy ace, Lt Cdr David McCampbell. Smith is see here after his return to *Wasp*, touching the US Navy wings awarded to him to commemorate the feat (*USN*)

FIRST DELIVERY

On 7 March 1942 Operation *Spotter* was mounted, which saw the first Spitfires delivered to Malta – it was also the first time that the fighter had deployed to a base outside the United Kingdom. At dawn, with 16 Mk VBs ranged on her deck, the aircraft carrier HMS *Eagle* reached the launch point off the coast of Algeria. These were dangerous waters, and a major fleet operation was necessary to protect the carrier, with her escorting force comprising a battleship, a cruiser, nine destroyers and the small carrier *Argus*. Sgt Jack

Jerry Smith prepares to make his second take-off from *Wasp* as the carrier nears Gibraltar after her second delivery operation. Smith finally reached Malta from HMS *Eagle* during Operation *LB* on 18 May. This determined pilot served with No 126 Sqn once on the besieged island, and was killed in action in August. Smith was credited with 3 enemy aircraft destroyed, 1 and 1 shared probably destroyed and 4 damaged (USN)

'Slim' Yarra, an Australian destined later to become a fighter ace over Malta, described the take-off in his diary;

'When the time came – 7 am on the second day out – everyone was keyed up and expectant and most of us were wondering if the Spitfires would really get off the deck quite OK. . . All the aircraft were lined up waiting and everyone was in their cockpits a full half hour before the first Blenheim, which was to lead us there, arrived. The Blenheim was sighted and the ship turned into wind. The first motor started and was run up. Suddenly the naval controller signalled "Chocks Away" and Sqn Ldr Grant (Sqn Ldr Stanley Grant, who also went on to achieve ace status on Malta, Ed.) opened his throttle and went roaring down the deck. He lifted off the end, sank slightly below the level of the deck, and sailed away, gaining altitude and proving that a Spitfire can take-off from an aircraft carrier.'

The rest of the Spitfires followed Grant into the air except for one – Jack Yarra's machine was unserviceable and remained on the deck. Those that got airborne all reached Malta safely, and after landing at Takali they were assigned to No 249 Sqn. A few days later Sqn Ldr Grant, who had led the Spitfires to Malta, assumed command of the squadron.

Spitfires went into action over Malta for the first time on 10 March, claiming one enemy aircraft destroyed, two probably destroyed and one damaged. In return, one of the new fighters was destroyed and another suffered damage. The Spitfire's main role on Malta was to provide top cover for the slower Hurricanes, thus allowing the latter to engage the bombers with less risk of coming under attack from Messerschmitts.

The aerial bombardment of the island continued without pause, and

Mk VC BP955/J-1 was flown by No 601 Sqn's Flt Lt Denis Barnham from Luqa, Malta, in April 1942 – both Barnham and this aircraft had earlier flown to the island as part of Operation *Calendar*. Twenty-four hours after his arrival he used this aircraft to probably destroy a Ju 88. The Spitfire was lost in action in October 1942. At the end of the war Barnham's victory score was 5 and 1 shared destroyed, 1 probably destroyed and 1 damaged

the Spitfire force dwindled rapidly as aircraft were destroyed or damaged in the air or on the ground. A further delivery run by *Eagle* on 21 March yielded nine more Spitfires, but these failed to replace the losses suffered in the intervening fortnight as only two aircraft out of the fifteen originally delivered remained airworthy.

The ferocious air fighting over Malta continued unabated, and by the evening of 23 March the defenders were left with just five serviceable Spitfires and Hurricanes.

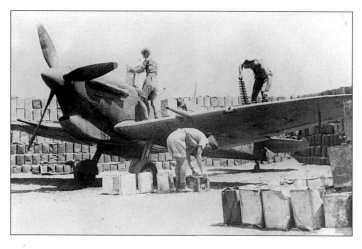

Five days later *Eagle* delivered another seven Spitfires, but from then on the island's future looked bleak indeed as the vessel – the only way to deliver fighters to replace those lost – suffered damage to her steering gear and required four weeks in dock for urgent repairs. The Royal Navy had no other carrier available that could bring in more fighters.

Meanwhile, April 1942 saw the air attacks on Malta rise to a crescendo, with some 5500 tons of bombs falling on the island and causing extensive damage. During the first half of the month it was a rare day when more than six RAF fighters took off to harry the raiders, the surviving RAF bombers, torpedo-bombers and submarines being forced to leave Malta and head for Gibraltar or Egypt – to remain in place without adequate fighter cover would have meant their almost certain destruction.

A soldier, a sailor and an airman carry out the refuelling and rearming of a Mk VC of No 603 Sqn in a makeshift revetment at Takali, Malta. Note that this aircraft has had the inner 20 mm cannon removed and the gun ports filled with locally made wooden bungs – its outer .303-in machine guns also appear to have been removed (*via Robertson*)

US ASSISTANCE

Meanwhile, the continued salvation of the battered island was discussed at the very highest level. Winston Churchill sent a personal telegram to President Roosevelt, asking if it might be possible to use the carrier USS *Wasp* to transport a batch of Spitfires to the island. The US President gave his assent, and on 10 April the American warship docked at Port Glasgow to take on the fighters. *Wasp* was much larger than *Eagle*, as shown by her

This trio of well-worn Mk Vs of No 249 Sqn were photographed at Takali, the aircraft nearest the camera, Mk VC BR130, being one of the aircraft delivered during *Calendar*. The fact that these fighters could sit out in the open in a line indicates that this photo was taken during a lull in the fighting in 1942

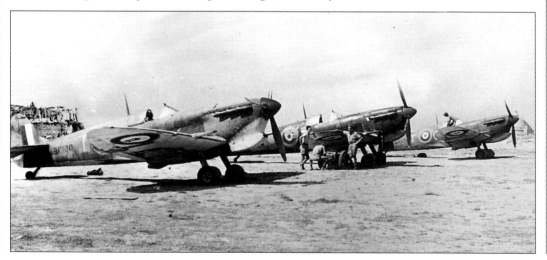

An ignominious end for a Mk VB of No 249 Sqn at Takali. The circumstances of the loss were not recorded

Sqn Ldr Percy 'Laddie' Lucas joined No 249 Sqn in March 1942, and was appointed commander of the unit three months later. His victory score, amassed while flying with the squadron, was 1 and 2 shared enemy aircraft destroyed, 1 probably destroyed and 8 and 1 shared damaged (*via Franks*)

ability to carry 47 Spitfire VCs in addition to 12 of her own Wildcat fighters for self-protection.

The delivery was code-named Operation *Calendar*, and on 13 April the American carrier set sail from the Scottish port. At first light on the 20th *Wasp* arrived at the fly-off point. Each Spitfire VC was fitted with four 20 mm cannon, although to save weight only two of them were loaded during the ferry flight. The first 12 Spitfires to launch were ranged on the after deck, with the remaining 35 lashed down in the ship's hangar. Once the aircraft on deck were airborne, those in the hangar started their engines and were brought up for launch by lift one at a time, before taking off immediately. In his book, *One Man's Window* (William Kimber 1956), Flt Lt Dennis Barnham (who also 'made ace' over Malta), a flight commander with No 601 Sqn, described his impressions of that memorable morning;

'Strapped tight (into BP969/R, Ed.) I can't look round. Glancing into the mirror above my windscreen, I observe that the Spitfire behind me, with the CO (Spitfire ace Sqn Ldr John Bisdee, who was shot down and wounded the very next day after downing a Ju 88, Ed.) inside, is being wheeled backwards towards the great lift – a pause – then, with the propeller turning in a transparent arc, the perspective of the plane changes as it disappears bodily, the floor with it, up into the blackness of the girders. Down comes the lift again and monkey-faced Scotty (Plt Off T W Scott, Ed.), one of our Australians, gives me a wide grin from the cockpit as his plane is dragged onto it. Down comes the empty floor again, hungry for more machines and their pilots. Up goes Max (Plt Off George M Briggs, also an Australian, who was killed in action on 10 May 1942, Ed.), it pauses in the roof, makes one gigantic swallow, then comes down again empty, this time for me.

'Mechanics grab my wings. I am pulled backwards toward the lift. Last glimpse of the hangar as the floor heaves beneath me: propellers turning, people running, a red sack has been thrown on to the floor down there. My God! Someone must have walked into a turning propeller. I'm on the deck in white daylight. Clouds, sea – flightdeck in front, the superstructure half way down the right. A white-sweatered American mechanic much too close, wearing goggles – a red skull cap on his head; I must watch him. With his legs apart, he's leaning forward like a rugger player, clenching his hands in the air. I put on the brakes. His hands being to rotate rapidly: I open the throttle. The engine is roaring, brakes are slipping. A checkered flag falls. Release brakes, throttle wide open, gathering speed, tail up, looking over the nose; –deck's very short. Going faster. The over-hanging bridge on the superstructure sweeps towards me; pink faces, pink blobs with no features on them – quick, wave goodbye to the Americans! Grab the stick again – end of the deck. Grey waves. Keep her straight – stick back. Out over the sea. Waves nearer. Stick further back – at last she begins to fly. Gaining more speed, I now start climbing. I don't suppose any enemy pilot could see the battleship, just below on my right, as close as this and survive. Changing on to the long range tank, I'm circling away to the left, climbing steadily. The engine does not falter, this is fine! With the ships looking like toys, I take position well to the left of the CO while the other three Spitfires which I have to lead clamber into formation behind me.

'As we set course toward the east, the sun rises out of the sea filling the whole of space with light.'

Of the 47 Spitfires that took off from *Wasp* that morning, all except one reached Malta. The sudden arrival of three squadrons-worth of Spitfires injected new life into the island's air defences, but the respite would prove short-lived. The airfields at Luqa and Takali, where the new arrivals were based, now came in for particularly heavy attacks. Several of the new fighters were destroyed or damaged on the ground, and Plt Off Mike 'Pancho' Le Bas, one of the pilots who had arrived with Barnham, described what happened;

'The Germans had watched our arrival on radar and that afternoon all Hell broke loosed over the Maltese airfields. In spite of strenuous efforts by the fighters and the anti-aircraft gun defences, the Ju 87 and Ju 88 dive-bombers and strafing Messerschmitts managed to damage and destroy several of the newly-delivered aircraft on the ground. The blast pens were made of local stone or stacks of petrol tins filled with sand, and they provided useful protection against cannon shells and blast from anything but a direct hit. They had no roofs, however, and several aircraft received damage when rocks blown high into the air by exploding bombs fell on them from above.'

By the morning of 21 April, only 27 of the Spitfires from *Wasp* were still flyable, and by that evening the number had fallen to 17 – one of the ten written off or damaged was BP955/J, which was crash-landed by Flt Lt Barnham after it had been hit in the engine by Bf 109s defending a formation of Ju 88s that had been attacked by No 601 Sqn. Meanwhile, in the island's repair workshops engineers struggled to assemble usable Spitfires and Hurricanes by cannibalising parts from more than a hundred damaged machines. As an example of their work, Barnham's aircraft was eventually returned to flight status, only to be eventually lost in action near Luqa on 17 October 1942 – its pilot, Sgt Ron Miller of No 229 Sqn, was never found.

The Spitfires delivered to Malta so far had been painted in sand and mid-stone camouflage, which made them less visible when they were on the ground or flying over land. However, when they were airborne the fighters spent much of their time over the sea, and in those colours they

Plt Off Rod Smith, brother of Jerry Smith who landed his Spitfire on *Wasp*, joined him on No 126 Sqn after arriving on Malta on 15 July 1942 as part of Operation *Pinpoint*. At the end of the war his victory score was 13 and 1 shared enemy aircraft destroyed, 1 shared probably destroyed and one damaged (*via Franks*)

Flt Lt John Plagis is seen in June 1942 whilst serving as a flight commander with No 185 Sqn at Krendi, Malta. By war's end his victory score stood at 15 enemy aircraft destroyed and 2 shared destroyed, 2 shared probably destroyed and 6 and 1 shared damaged (*via Sarkar*)

During the seige of Malta it required a major fleet operation by the Royal Navy to deliver even a small batch of new Spitfires to the island. Hence the vital importance of an effective repair and maintenance organisation on the island to keep as many of the available fighters as possible in full fighting trim. These Mk Vs are seen undergoing maintenance and repair at Gazan's garage, Valetta, which had been requisitioned specifically for this task (*via Robertson*)

Battle of France ace Sqn Ldr Maurice Stephens commanded No 229 Sqn at Takali in October and November 1942. At the end of the war his victory score was at least 17 and 3 shared destroyed, 1 probably destroyed and 5 damaged (*via Franks*)

showed up beautifully. To overcome this problem aircraft were repainted in the darker colours to make them less conspicuous, groundcrews using whatever paint was available locally, giving rise to a host of unofficial schemes. Later reinforcement Spitfires arrived in slate grey/dark green camouflage.

As April drew to a close, it was clear that despite the euphoria following Operation *Calendar*, Malta's survival was still in question. Yet again Prime Minister Churchill asked the US President for *Wasp* to deliver more Spitfires to the island, and yet again permission was forthcoming. The next resupply mission, Operation *Bowery*, was the largest of them all, the American carrier returning to Glasgow on 29 April and collecting another 47 Spitfires. Meanwhile HMS *Eagle*, lying at Gibraltar with the repairs to her steering gear completed, prepared to take 17 more.

As *Wasp* and her covering force passed through the Strait of Gibraltar, *Eagle* joined her and the two carriers headed together eastward into the Mediterranean. Shortly after dawn on 9 May they began launching their Spitfires – 64 in total. One fighter the 23rd launched) failed to get airborne when its pilot, Sgt R D Sherrington (a Canadian), inexplicably set its propeller in coarse pitch and the aircraft failed to attain take-off speed prior to running off the end of the deck. The fighter clipped the bows of the carrier as it ran off the edge and crashed into the sea, the vessel then slicing the stricken Spitfire in two, instantly killing the pilot.

A second pilot, Plt Off Jerry Smith, got airborne in BR126/3-X only to find that his drop tank would not deliver fuel, so the Canadian pilot orbited the carrier until the rest of the Spitfires had left. Then, rather than abandon his fighter, he decided to try to attempt a deck landing despite the fact that his aircraft lacked an arrester hook. After one balked attempt he made a reasonable landing, and with some harsh braking he halted the Spitfire just six feet short of the end of the deck – he had been guided back

aboard by Lt Cdr David McCampbell, who would later go on to to become the US Navy's leading ace in World War 2 (see Osprey volume *Aircraft of the Aces 10 Hellcat Aces of World War 2* for more details). Smith and his Spitfire remained on the carrier until it left the Mediterranean, then he took off again and landed at Gibraltar.

Of the 62 other Spitfires that left *Wasp* and *Eagle*, 60 reached Malta – two were lost when they collided whilst attacking an Italian Fiat RS 14 floatplane, which escaped unscathed. At Luqa, one of the pilots awaiting the arrival of the incoming fighters was Mike Le Bas;

'One of the problems when I had arrived (during Operation *Calendar*) was that the operation had been kept so secret that too few people had been told we were coming – the Spitfires had not been refuelled and rearmed quickly enough, with the result that they could not take-off to meet the attacks and several were knocked out on the ground. This time we were much better organised. As each Spitfire came in it was picked up at the end of the runway by a resident Malta pilot, who sat on the wing and guided the aircraft to its blast pen. At each pen there were waiting an RAF groundcrew and some soldiers to help with the refuelling. I guided one Spitfire in and, even before the pilot had shut down, men were clambering on the wings to load the cannon with their full complement of ammunition and soldiers had started a human chain to pass up the petrol tins. The pilot pulled off his helmet and shouted to me "That's jolly good. Where's the war?" I told him "The war hasn't started for you yet, mate. Get out and be quick about it!"'

Fifteen minutes after it landed, with the drop tank removed, the internal tanks refilled and the other two cannon re-armed, the Spitfire was

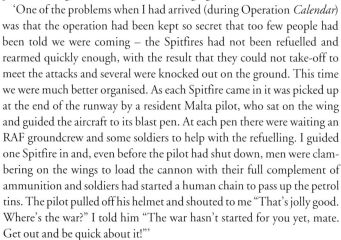

Italian Air Force officers examine BR112/X of No 185 Sqn after it crash landed on the beach at Scoglitti, Sicily, on 9 September 1942. Its pilot, Sgt Claude Weaver (an American who had joined the RCAF in early 1941), was taken prisoner. This aircraft was one of those delivered as part of Operation *Calendar* in April 1942, its blue paint scheme, hastily applied over the fighter's original desert camouflage once on Malta, clearly showing signs of pealing away. Following the Italian armistice Weaver escaped from captivity and resumed combat flying at the end of 1943, only to be killed in action shortly afterwards. At the time of his death his victory score was 12 and 1 shared destroyed and 3 probably destroyed

Mk VC BR498/PP-H was flown by Wg Cdr Peter Prosser Hanks, OC Luqa Wing, this aircraft having been delivered to Malta via HMS *Eagle* during one of the July reinforcement operations. Peter Hanks was flying it on 11 October 1942 when he was credited with the destruction of one Bf 109 and having damaged a second. The Spitfire remained in service until it was struck off charge in September 1945. At the end of the war Hanks's victory score was 13 and 1 and 3 shared probably destroyed and 6 damaged (*via Thomas*)

ready for action. Le Bas climbed in the cockpit and shortly afterwards was scrambled to meet an incoming raid.

SECURE DEFENCE

In the days that followed there were several ferocious air actions, but the arrival of the new batch of fighters meant that at last Malta had enough modern fighters to defend herself. Instead of the token force available at the beginning of May, she now had five full squadrons of Spitfires (Nos 126, 185, 249, 601 and 603 Sqns).

Soon afterwards, two events occurred to ensure that the reversal in the island's air defence fortunes was not a temporary abberation. First, the Luftwaffe strength on Sicily dropped sharply following the decision to abandon the plan to invade Malta. Some *Gruppen* went to the Eastern Front whilst others were sent to Libya, for in both theatres the Germans were assembling forces for powerful new offensives. Secondly, the delivery of Spitfires to Malta continued unabated – between 18 May and 9 June HMS *Eagle* made three more runs, which brought a further 76 Spitfires. From now on Malta had sufficient Spitfires to deal harshly with any

A Mk VB is taxies out at the commencement of a direct flight from North Front, Gibraltar, to Malta. The distance covered was 1100 miles, equivalent to that from London to St Petersburg, in Russia. The aircraft has had its armament removed, apart from two machine guns, and it carries a 170 gallon ferry tank under the fuselage, a 29 gallon addition tank in the rear fuselage and a deepened nose section to accommodate an enlarged oil tank. During September and October 1942 17 Spitfires set out from Gibraltar to fly to Malta – all except one made it (*RAF Museum*)

Sqn Ldr Joseph Lynch, OC No 249 Sqn at Krendi, is pictured on 28 April 1943 soon after shooting down the Ju 52 which was recorded as the 1000th enemy aircraft destroyed by the defences of Malta. At the end of the war Lynch's victory score was 10 and 7 shared destroyed, 1 probably destroyed and 1 shared damaged (*via Robertson*)

attacks mounted by the German and Italian Air Forces. Never again would the islanders face as great a peril from air attack as during that first week in May 1942.

The seizure of air superiority over Malta had important implications for the strategy of the war in the Mediterranean. Following the withdrawal of Malta's anti-shipping forces and submarines in April, Axis convoys had plied between Italy and North Africa almost without hindrance. That made possible the rapid build-up of supplies in Libya in preparation for the new German offensive there, but now that situation had changed. With an adequate air defence restored, the anti-shipping units could return to Malta, and at the beginning of June these squadrons resumed their debilitating attacks on Axis supply convoys.

In June the air attacks on Malta tailed off, but the new German offensive in North Africa made rapid initial gains. The air commander on the island felt secure enough to pass on one of his precious Spitfire squadrons to Egypt where there was greater need for it, so on 23 June the fighters of No 601 Sqn had their ferry tanks refitted and the unit re-deployed to

Spitfire Vs of No 249 Sqn are seen on patrol off Malta in 1943. The leading aircraft and that on the left have clip wings, whilst the remaining pair have standard-span wings (*Kennedy*)

Mk V BR586/T-M of No 249 Sqn, pictured in July 1943. This aircraft survived the war and was one of a batch passed to the Royal Hellenic Air Force in 1946 (*via Thomas*)

Mersa Matruh. The flight of just over 800 miles – the longest yet made by Spitfire fighters – took $4^{1}/2$ hours.

Even that was not the limit of the fighter's ferry range, however, for in the summer of 1942 Supermarine engineers completed the development of a 170-gallon ferry tank for the Spitfire. Together with an auxiliary tank in the rear fuselage, which held 29 gallons, the additional fuel cells gave the fighter a total load of 284 gallons. This was sufficient to allow the aircraft to cover the 1100 miles from Gibraltar to Malta in one hop, and still leave a reasonable reserve. Now Spitfires could be delivered to the island when required, without the need for a major naval operation involving an aircraft carrier and a large escorting force.

The first direct flight of Spitfires from Gibraltar to Malta – Operation *Train* – took place on 25 October, and between then and the end of November 1942, 15 more Spitfires set out to make the flight – all except one made it. The $5^{1}/2$-hour flight was a remarkable feat for an aircraft designed originally as a short-range interceptor, the still-air distance covered being about as far as from London to St Petersburg, in Russia.

Had more Spitfires been required in Malta, they too would have flown to the island direct, but the rapid Allied advance into Libya following the victory at El Alamein brought an end to the siege of the island. The part played by Spitfire Vs in this action, and others elsewhere in the Mediterranean area, is described in Chapter Six, but first, let us take a closer look at the nature of the air fighting over Malta, and the tactics employed by Spitfire units.

DELIVERIES OF SPITFIRES TO MALTA BY AIRCRAFT CARRIER IN 1942

Date	Operation	Carrier	Took Off	Arrived
7 March	*Spotter*	HMS *Eagle*	15	15
21 March	*Picket I*	HMS *Eagle*	9	9
29 March	*Picket II*	HMS *Eagle*	7	7
20 April	*Calendar*	USS *Wasp*	47	46
9 May	*Bowery*	USS *Wasp*	64	60
		HMS *Eagle*		
18 May	*LB*	HMS *Eagle*	17	17
3 June	*Style*	HMS *Eagle*	31	27
9 June	*Salient*	HMS *Eagle*	32	32
15 July	*Pinpoint*	HMS *Eagle*	32	31
21 July	*Insect*	HMS *Eagle*	30	28
11 August	*Bellows*	HMS *Furious*	38	37
17 August	*Baritone*	HMS *Furious*	32	29
24 October	*Train*	HMS *Furious*	31	29

TACTICS OF A MALTA ACE

Plt Off Reade F Tilley was an American who joined the RCAF before his country entered the war. Having completed his training, he flew Spitfire VBs for a time with No 121 'Eagle' Sqn – he claimed a Fw 190 probable on a sweep over France on 24 March 1942, this being his sole claim whilst flying on the Channel front. The following month he was posted to No 601 Sqn shortly before the unit went to Malta, and on 20 April he took off from USS *Wasp* in one of the Spitfires delivered to the island during Operation *Calendar*.

Once on the island, Tilley quickly transferred to No 126 Sqn, and subsequently flew with the veteran Malta unit for four months during some of the heaviest air fighting of the entire campaign. During that period he amassed a score of seven enemy aircraft destroyed, two probably destroyed and six damaged, and was awarded the DFC. In August he left the island and transferred to the USAAF's Eighth Fighter Command.

After completing a staff posting, Tilley returned to the USA and entered the training organisation, tasked with passing his combat experience to officers earmarked to command new fighter units being formed. To assist with this he wrote a lengthy tactical paper, describing the practical lessons he had learned while flying over Malta. Excerpts from his paper are given below;

'When fighters are scrambled to intercept an approaching enemy, every minute wasted in getting off the ground and forming up means 3000 ft of altitude you won't have when you need it most. Thus an elaborate cockpit check is out. It is sufficient to see that you are in fine pitch and the motor is running properly before opening the throttle. Don't do a Training School circuit before joining up. As you roll down the runway take a quick look up for the man off ahead of you, and when you have sufficient indicated air speed give him about six rings of deflection (on the gunsight) and you will be alongside in a flash. Don't jam open the throttle and follow along behind as it takes three times as long to catch up that way. If you are leading, circle the drome close in, throttled well back, waggling your wings like Hell.

'The instant you are in formation get the cockpit in "fighting shape": trimmed for the climb, oxygen right, check engine instruments, gun button to fire. Now you are ready for action. If something is wrong *now* is the time to go back. Waggle your wings then slide gently out of the formation, or if following break sharply down and go home. *Never* wait until you are in the vicinity of enemy aircraft then make a break for it on a last minute decision. There are several reasons for this:

A. The leader may be depending on you.

B. The rest of the formation may think you are diving on the enemy and follow you (this has happened before and it plays Hell with everything).

American Plt Off Reade Tilley, DFC, joined the RCAF in 1940 and flew with No 121 'Eagle' Sqn for several months, during which time he claimed an Fw 190 probably destroyed. In April 1942 he was posted to No 601 Sqn and flew a Spitfire to Malta as part of Operation *Calendar*. After a few days on the island he transferred to No 126 Sqn, and in the weeks that followed his score built up steadily. Early in June he was flown to Gibraltar, where he boarded HMS *Eagle* to lead a new batch of Spitfires to the island as part of Operation *Salient*. In August 1942 he left the island to transfer to the USAAF. At that time his score stood at 7 destroyed, 3 probably destroyed and 6 damaged (*Tilley*)

Section of four aircraft giving mutual cover, to scale
(Shading indicates blind zones.)

C. The enemy may spot you and take advantage of your solitude.'

At this stage of the war the RAF used the section 'fours line abreast' battle formation, similar to the *Schwarm* employed by the Luftwaffe, with aircraft flying about 80 yards apart. A squadron comprised three such sections, typically with Red Section in the lead with White and Blue Sections to the left and right of it, slightly above and 500-700 yards behind. Tilley continued;

'Squadron commanders must bear in mind that the squadron must be intact to do maximum damage to the enemy in combat; to this end throttle back and even turn towards straggling sections while climbing to meet the enemy. There is no better feeling than to arrive at 25,000 ft with the full squadron properly deployed and then start hunting.

'In sections "fours line abreast" each aircraft watches the others' tails, above and below, and in doing so all four cover each other.

'The arrows indicate the direction in which the pilots keep watch. When everyone does his job it is impossible for an enemy aircraft to get into a firing position without being seen by at least three out of the four pilots. On a larger scale, the sections cover each other. Any section that is being attacked will be covered by the next section; and the pay-off is that the enemy frequently sees only one or two sections, and in attacking or manoeuvring they lay themselves wide open to the attentions of the third section.

'One further advantage of this formation is that if one man is attacked, the man next to him is at the exact distance where he can throttle back and fire at the attacker from the beam. Moreover, the sections are at the exact distance apart so that they are in effective range of any aircraft who is within range astern of one of the others.'

Good radio communications were (and, indeed, still are) essential if fighters are to carry out co-ordinated, and therefore effective, operations. Tilley devoted a large section in his tactical paper to the proper use of radio in combat, and pointed to several pitfalls that remain relevant to the present day;

'Forget all the fancy pleasantries you learned to put before and after the message in voice radio procedure. In your business there is no

Reade Tilley looks on from the cockpit of a No 126 Sqn Spitfire VB at Takali as his groundcrew service the fighter between sorties

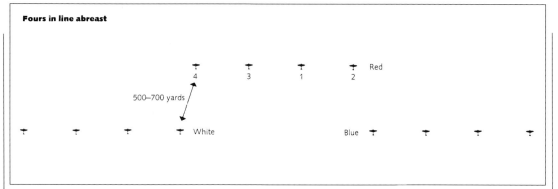

Fours in line abreast

500–700 yards

4   3   1   2   Red

White   Blue

time for it and the message is the important thing. The squadron leader is the only man who uses the R/T for transmission when the squadron is in pursuit of the Germans. There is no need for you to say anything, just keep your mouth shut and reflect on the ground controller's messages to the leader. You will learn all you need to know: how many of the enemy to expect, at what altitude and from what direction they are approaching. The leader acknowledges the messages from the ground controller with a sharp "OK". That is all that is necessary unless several squadrons or sections are operating independently, in which case "Red Leader OK" or "Blue Leader answering OK" is sufficient. The latter message takes $2^{1}/_{2}$ seconds; until the enemy is sighted no transmission should be longer. If a 4- or 5-second message about nothing in particular is in progress, when everyone suddenly realises that the wingman is being fired at by a Focke-Wulf, then no one can warn him until the message is completed and he probably won't be interested by then. It's amazing how many holes can be punched in an airplane in four or five seconds . . .

'So keep your eyes open and your mouth shut until you spot the enemy, then your moment has come. If they are far ahead, or off to one side or below and far away from you, there is plenty of time; don't get excited, just sit there and look them over – it doesn't help much if you report Spitfires as '109s. Try to count them or make a rapid estimate (for your log book). If you recognise them, give their identity; if not, report them as "aircraft". The procedure: make your voice purposely calm, slow and unexcited: "Hello Red Leader; '109s at 4 o'clock above" or "Red 3 to Red Leader; aircraft at 9 o'clock our level".

'Red Leader sees the aircraft and acknowledges "OK". Now above all leave the R/T clear, for the next words will be you leader's instruction. If these are jammed it may queer the whole set-up.

'Sometimes enemy aircraft are not seen until they are actually attacking. *Then the message must be instantaneous and precise.* If it is incoherent or garbled because you are excited the man being attacked may get a cannon shell instead – and first. The proper procedure: "'109's attacking Red Section" or if you see one man being fired at "Look out Red 4" or "Red 4 break" – any one of these messages spoken clearly is perfect. Just be sure you designate the man being attacked correctly. It doesn't help much if you tell Red 4 to break (which he does) while Red 2, who is being fired at, looks on admiringly.

'The one sure way to lose friends and help the enemy is to give a panic message over the R/T at the critical moment. "Look out, there's a '109 on your tail!", said in a screech, is usually sufficient to send every Spitfire within a radius of 50 miles into a series of wild manoeuvres. There is no

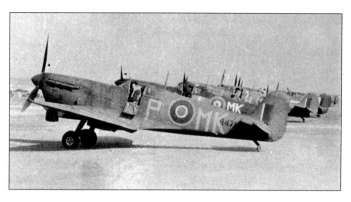

Mk Vs of No 126 Sqn are seen at Luqa following the unit's move there in May 1942. The aircraft nearest the camera, ER471, arrived in Malta early in 1943 and survived to the end of the war

call sign, so every pilot in every squadron responds automatically. Far better to say nothing at all and let one pilot be shot down, than break up several formations for Jerry to pick off at his leisure. In fighter flying, a panic message is the greatest of all crimes . . .

'If your R/T packs up near base, go back; if near the enemy, stay with the unit. A fighter pilot without R/T is a liability to himself and his squadron. Never take-off with a faulty RT.'

Tilley went on to outline some of the survival lessons he had learned during his time in the hard school of combat;

'Enemy aircraft do not fly alone. They fly in pairs or fours. If you can see just one, have a damn good look round for his pal before you go in to attack . . . and remember, *look out behind!*

'When you attack, a series of two or three second bursts with a new aim and angle of deflection each time is the most effective. Don't cease attacking just because the enemy aircraft is beginning to smoke or a few pieces fall off; then is the time to skid out for a good look behind, before closing in to point blank range and really giving it to him.

'When actually firing at the enemy aircraft you are most vulnerable to attack. When you break away from an attack, *always* break with a violent skid just as though you were being fired at from behind – because maybe you are!

'It would seem reasonable to suppose that the straggler in a fighter formation would be the last man to get home – but he rarely is! Play hard to get, don't straggle, *and look out behind, always!*

Tilley considered the Ju 88 to be the most formidable enemy bomber type he encountered over Malta, and he afforded it considerable respect – he succeeded in shooting one down on 9 July 1942. These aircraft were capable of making highly accurate dive-bombing attacks on airfields and other targets, and were much feared;

'When '88s are permitted to operate without fighter interference they can place 6000 lbs (short range load) of explosive in a 100 yd square, every time . . . The '88s normally approach the target area at 17,000 ft. They fly in sections of three in vee with other sections in line astern. The general form is German fighters arrive over the target a few minutes before the raid, flying in loose pairs or fours. Their job is to break up any fighter formation in the vicinity. The Big Jobs come in with a close escort and a high cover escort that may be anywhere up to 30,000 (ft). The dive is usually made out of the sun to fox the ground defences, but if there is no intensive ground fire they prefer to dive up wind. They come down at about 60° releasing bombs at about 6000 (ft) and breaking away with a steep turn, in line astern.'

In Tilley's view the best way to counter this type of attack was to engage the bombers before they began their attack dives;

'The procedure is to divide your fighter strength. Half patrol just up-sun from the target at about 15,000 (ft) while the other force goes out at 20,000 or more in an effort to intercept the bombers and break them up.

Sometimes when intercepted they jettison their bombs and scatter, all heading for home. But if the target is vital they are more likely to continue on regardless. Always attack '88s from head-on when possible. A few fighters can absolutely wreck a large '88 formation by going through it head-on. The fire from the front gunner is ineffective and the close escort fighters are helpless. To execute the attack effectively, throttle fully back and aim at the lead bomber. Open fire at 600 yards and hold your burst right up to his props.'

Once Ju 88s had commenced their attack dives, the defending fighters had to try to engage them on the way down;

''88s come down in line astern, about 500 yards apart. The procedure: dive straight for that line and each fighter joins in behind an '88. The rear gunner is firing at an awkward angle and the (bomber's) pilot must dive in a dead straight line, so close in to point blank range and put steady bursts into one engine. If you notice tracer from the rear it is likely to be the front gunner of the '88 behind trying to make you think he's a '109. Once you have set an '88 on fire, skid out – *take a good look behind for fighters* – then throttle back and attack the next in line from the beam.'

When he broke off the combat, the fighter pilot's concerns did not end. If his aircraft had suffered damage, it was important to learn its nature as soon as possible and take action to limit its effect;

'The first action after combat is not to shake hands with yourself but to look at the engine instruments. Dropping oil pressure and rising engine and oil temperatures mean trouble. If you have been hit in the radiator or the glycol pipes, white smoke starts to flow immediately. This is usually visible from the cockpit. If you have had bad luck the main glycol feed pipe running alongside the cockpit may be ruptured, in which case the cockpit will be filled with hot glycol and dense white vapour which causes choking and blindness. There is no hope to save an aircraft so hit. If, however, the glycol smoke is outside then open the hood, turn the oxygen to emergency and land at the nearest drome. If you have a long way to go to reach your lines or the coast, throttle well back in course pitch and prepare to get out or crash land should the engine quit.

'A hit through the oil piping or motor block is not so obvious, though it will show on your oil pressure and engine instruments immediately. Often it is possible to cover a good many miles well throttled back in coarse pitch before the engine seizes. When your aircraft starts trailing heavy smoke it may catch fire at any moment so watch for the first sign of flame; if it appears, bale out immediately as an explosion may follow without further warning.

'The only way you can't get out of a Spitfire is to climb out. The best method, if you have time, is to roll over on your back, trim her a bit tail heavy then pull (the locking pin from the safety harness). If you are in a hurry (and sometimes this is the case) just pull the pin and jam the stick forward; your last sensation will be your fingers leaving the stick. This works with the aircraft in any position. If the hood is jammed shut and you can't open it (sometimes a bullet or a shell may foul the track) lower the seat to the bottom, pull the pin, stiffen the neck and back muscles, then give the stick one Hell of a shove forward. You won't even notice the hood . . .

'*LOOK OUT BEHIND*, then all of this won't be necessary.'

NORTH AFICA

Following the initial deliveries of Spitfires to Malta, the next theatre earmarked to receive these fighters was North Africa. During April 1942 the personnel for two Spitfire squadrons, Nos 92 and No 145, arrived in Egypt. Malta still had first call on the tropical-modified Spitfires, however, and her needs proved greater than expected – they were met by diverting fighters from the two units sent to Egypt.

The delivery route of short range aircraft to Egypt was even more difficult than that to Malta, crated aircraft being shipped to the port of Takoradi, in the Gold Coast (now Ghana), where they were re-assembled and test flown. They then flew along the trans-African reinforcement route to Egypt, with ten hops that took them through Nigeria, French Equatorial Africa and the Sudan.

It was the latter part of May before No 145 Sqn received its full complement of fighters, the unit then re-deploying to a forward landing ground near Gambut, in eastern Libya. On 1 June it flew its first combat mission in the theatre when it provided top cover for Hurricanes engaged in a ground strafing mission. In the meantime, however, the German and Italian forces had launched a large scale offensive and were making rapid progress eastward. British and Commonwealth forces were forced back steadily as position after position was overrun, and soon after the Spitfire unit arrived at Gambut, it had to beat a hasty retreat to Landing Ground 155 near Sidi Barrani, in western Egypt. On 10 June, during hectic aerial fighting over the battle area, the squadron OC, Sqn Ldr Charles Overton, finally achieved ace status when he shot down a II./JG 27 Bf 109F near Bir Hacheim – this aircraft was being flown at the time by 39-kill ace Oberleutenant Rudolf Sinner (see Osprey volume *Aircraft of the Aces 2 Bf 109 Aces of the Mediterranean and North Africa* for more details). Overton's tally had been stuck on 4½ kills since 13 August 1940! Soon Sidi Barrani came under threat too, and the squadron had to pull back again, this time to LG 154 near Alexandria.

BR114 was one of the Mk Vs modified into high altitude fighters at No 103 Maintenance Unit, Aboukir, to engage high-flying Junkers Ju 86P reconnaissance aircraft. Externally, the non-standard points to note are the four-bladed propeller, the absence of the radio mast, a toughened glass windscreen, the rubbed down and polished areas of the surface at the joints and pointed wing tips which increased the wing area (*via Thomas*)

The Axis advance was finally halted at El Alamein, within 60 miles of Alexandria, on 25 June. By that time two Spitfire squadrons were operational at LG 154 – No 145, as already mentioned, and No 601, which had just arrived from Malta (see Chapter Four). No 92 Sqn was still awaiting its full complement of aircraft.

During the heavy fighting of the past few weeks, fighter units equipped with Hurricanes and Kittyhawks had suffered at the hands of the faster Bf 109Fs. More Spitfires were desperately needed in the theatre, and they would arrive from an unexpected source – on 2 July the freighter *Nigerstown*, carrying 42 Spitfire Vs intended for Australia, was part of a convoy that put in to Freetown in Sierra Leone. The freighter, with its valuable cargo, was immediately 'high-jacked' and sent to Takoradi, where the fighters were off-loaded and hastily assembled. They then set off on the trans-Africa route, the first of them reaching Egypt before the end of the month. These surprise arrivals were pressed into service with No 92 Sqn, bringing the unit to full strength, whilst the remaining Spitfires formed a reserve in order to replace losses incurred by the three squadrons.

Mk VB of No 145 Sqn, the first Spitfire fighter unit to become operational over the Western Desert (*via Franks*)

HIGH ALTITUDE INTERLUDE

In the spring and summer of 1942 Ju 86P reconnaissance aircraft based in Crete flew several ultra-high altitude photographic missions over British military installations in Egypt. This advanced aircraft was powered by two Jumo 207 diesel engines with two-stage superchargers, and had a pressurized cabin for its two-man crew.

A typical mission was that flown on 20 August, Allied radars tracking a Ju 86P crossing the coast near Port Said at 40,000 ft. Cruising at a sedate 200 mph, it flew down the entire length of the Suez Canal photographing shipping, military bases and airfields along the waterway. Then it headed north-west to photograph the fighter landing grounds near Alexandria

Mk VC BR392 was one of the Spitfires bound for Australia on the freighter *Nigerstown* when it was 'highjacked' in July 1942 and diverted to the Middle East. It was duly issued to No 601 Sqn, and eventually lost in action in the following October

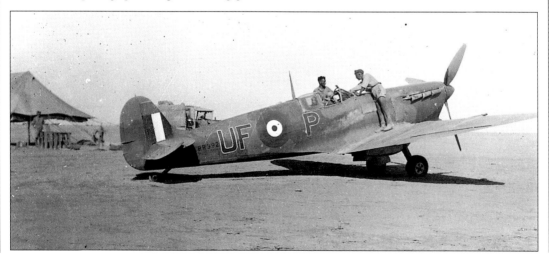

American Sqn Ldr Lance 'Wildcat'
Wade joined the RAF before his
country entered the war, and
subsequently amassed a large
victory score flying Hurricanes in the
Western Desert in 1941-42. In
January 1943 he was given
command of No 145 Sqn, flying Mk
Vs during the campaign in Tunisia.
Wade was killed in a flying accident
in 1944 when his score stood at 22
and 2 shared destroyed, 1 probably
destroyed and 13 damaged

Flt Lt John Taylor served with No
145 Sqn in the Western Desert in the
summer of 1942. In March 1943 he
was promoted and assumed
command of No 601 Sqn, but was
killed in action in the following July.
At the time of his death his victory
score stood at 13 and 2 shared
destroyed, 2 probably destroyed and
10 and 2 shared damaged
(*via Franks*)

(including, no doubt, LG 154) before passing over the naval base and
heading out to sea. Five Spitfires went after the intruder and two fired
bursts at it from well below its altitude, but neither claimed hits. Aerial
reconnaissance was not a one-sided business, however, for the long range
reconnaissance version of the Spitfire – the Mk IV – was also active in this
theatre. Although it lacked the ultra-high altitude performance of the
German aircraft, it was much faster, and also operated with similar
immunity over Axis-held areas.

The need to halt, or at least hinder, the Ju 86P's photographic operations soon became a matter of the utmost military importance. The
British army was dug in along the 'last ditch line' at El Alamein, and German Gen Erwin Rommel was preparing a major offensive to penetrate
that line. Throughout this period the Ju 86Ps were able to run line cover-
age of large parts of the British defences and rear areas at regular intervals.

In a bid to counter the menace, half a dozen Spitfire VI high altitude
fighters had arrived in Egypt, but with its weighty pressurised cabin, this
variant was too heavy to reach the altitudes attained by the Ju 86P. Engineers at No 103 Maintenance Unit at Aboukir therefore decided to mod-
ify a few Mk Vs into high altitude interceptors, stripping all unnecessary
equipment, including the armour and the four .303-in machine guns, in
order to lighten the aircraft. The engines were also modified to give an
increased compression ratio, and each fighter was fitted with a four-
bladed propeller taken from a Spitfire VI. At least three fighters – BP985,
BR114 and BR234 – were modified in this way, also being fitted with
pointed wing tips and an armament of two .5-in machine guns instead of
the 20 mm cannon.

At this point it is necessary to digress in order to explain the effect of the
height of the stratosphere on a Spitfire's performance. At altitudes below
the stratosphere, the air temperature decreases at a steady rate as altitude
is increased. Once the stratosphere is reached, however, as altitude is
increased the temperature remains reasonably constant over the next
10,000 ft or so. The nearer to the equator, the greater the height of the
stratosphere. As Cairo lies at 30° North, the stratosphere in this region
commences at about 45,000 ft, and above that altitude the air temperature remains steady at about -62°C. Moving further from the equator, the
stratosphere gets lower and the layer of air above it is a little less cold. Thus
over London, at 52° North, the height of the stratosphere is about 36,000
ft and above it the air temperature is about -54°C.

Differences in the outside air temperature at high altitude had a marked
effect on the performance of the Spitfire V. The colder the air drawn into
its carburettor, the greater its density and therefore the greater the power
developed by the Merlin engine. Thus a Spitfire flying over Egypt had a
substantially higher service ceiling than if it was flying over the United
Kingdom.

The stripped-down Spitfire had their first success on 24 August when
Flg Off G Reynolds intercepted a Ju 86P north of Cairo at about 37,000
ft. At first the intruder tried to outclimb the fighter, but after a long chase
which took him up to 42,000 ft, Reynolds closed to 150 yards and
opened fire. He thought he had scored hits on the starboard engine, after
which the Junkers banked away and he lost contact. Several published
accounts state that the Ju 86P was destroyed in this encounter, yet Ger-

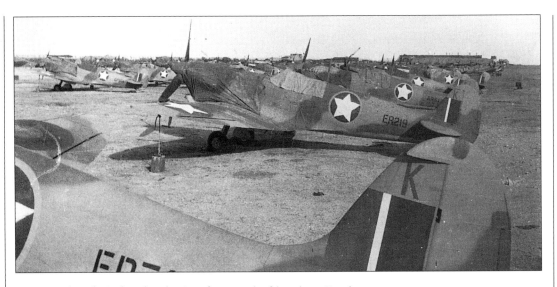

man records make it clear that the aircraft returned safely to base. For the Luftwaffe crews, however, it was a clear portent that their long immunity from fighter interception was coming to an end.

Following that initial action, the high altitude Spitfires underwent further modifications to reduce their weight, with the radios and associated masts being removed, a lightweight battery fitted in place of the normal one and the fuel load reduced by 30 gallons. Under a revised tactical plan for high altitude interceptions, this suitably-modified aircraft became the so-called 'Striker', and accompanying it during the interception would be another lightened Spitfire fitted with a radio, called the 'Marker'. Its pilot was in radio contact with the ground controller, and he followed the latter's intercept vectors to bring him as close as possible to the enemy aircraft. The pilot of the 'Striker' was to maintain position several thousand feet above and to one side of the 'Marker' until he caught sight of the Ju 86P, then he could move in to engage it. If he could inflict damage with his limited armament, he might force the Junkers to descend so that the 'Marker' could attack also.

The new tactics were tested in action for the first time on 29 August 1942 when Plt Off George Genders (already an ace with 7$\frac{1}{2}$ kills from his previous North Africa tour with No 33 Sqn on Hurricanes) in the 'Striker' reached a position about 1000 ft below the Junkers but could only fire a brief burst before his guns jammed. After the engagement he made no claim, but from German records we know that that burst was more effective than he had thought. The Ju 86P had suffered serious damage which forced its crew to ditch in the Mediterranean – the latter were picked up by the German rescue service.

On 6 September Plt Off George Genders was again flying the 'Striker' – BR234 on this occasion –

A total of 274 Spitfire Vs were delivered to the US Twelfth Air Force under reverse lend-lease, and served with the 31st and 52nd Fighter Groups during the campaigns in Tunisia and Sicily. These aircraft are seen parked at North Front, Gibraltar, in November 1942, awaiting issue to US units. They are all camouflaged in the standard RAF desert scheme of mid-stone and brown. Note the crudely painted star markings painted over the RAF roundels (*RAF Museum*)

During the campaign in Tunisia Allied units were sometimes forced to operate from ill-equipped airfields and under atrocious conditions. This Mk V, VF-E of the 5th FS/52nd FG, sits in axle-deep rain water at its dispersal (*via Thomas*)

when he intercepted a Ju 86P at high altitude and pursued it out to sea. The reconnaissance aircraft was about 80 miles north of Alexandria before he finally reached an attacking position. His rounds damaged the Junkers, forcing its crew to descend, whereupon Plt Off A Gold in the 'Marker' delivered further attacks. The Ju 86P was last seen heading out over the Mediterranean and the pilots claimed it as dam-

Mk VC of the 308th FS/31st FG. The aircraft carries the code HL-AA, the AA identifying it as the aircraft flown by Lt Col R A Ames, the group's Executive Officer (*via Robertson*)

aged. That long tail chase had depleted the 'Striker's' limited fuel supply, however, and on the way home Genders ran out. He continued south in a glide, but when the aircraft reached 1000 ft and he was still short of the coast, Genders bailed out. The pilot came down in the sea and, after an air-sea search had failed to locate him, he finally swam ashore after 21 hours in the water. From German records we know that this Ju 86P also failed to survive the encounter, crash landing in a German-held area of desert and being declared a total loss.

There were two further interceptions of Ju 86Ps in September, on the 10th by Fg Off Reynolds and on the 15th by Plt Off Gold. Both pilots opened fire at the intruder and thought they might have scored hits, but German records do not mention a Ju 86P suffering damage on either day.

In fact, the modified Spitfire Vs had done sufficient to curtail further reconnaissance sorties. During the final week of July the German reconnaissance unit had three Ju 86Ps on strength, of which only one was serviceable – despite this aircraft's impressive performance, its poor serviceability record held down the sortie rate. By destroying two Ju 86Ps in the space of eight days, the Spitfires ended their more brazen incursions into the Nile delta area. From then on the high-flying reconnaissance aircraft flew only occasionally, and when they did they avoided well-defended areas.

EL ALAMEIN AND AFTER

During the ferocious air actions that accompanied the ground battles at El Alamein, the Spitfire unit's main task was to provide top cover so that other RAF units could perform their duties without being molested. That role frequently placed the Spitfires in confrontation with the German Bf 109Fs.

The three Spitfire units within the Western Desert Air Force at that time were grouped together in No 244 Wing. After the long and frustrating wait for its aircraft, the last of this initial trio, No 92 Sqn, re-entered the fight with a vengeance under the leadership of Battle of Britain veteran, Sqn Ldr Jefferson Wedgwood. Indeed, the OC opened the unit's score in-theatre on 14 August 1942 when he shot down a II./JG 27 Bf 109F. Between then and the end of October he was credited with a further seven Bf 109s destroyed, plus a similar number damaged (and a solitary damaged against a Ju 87). Flt Lt John Morgan was another high scorer with the squadron, being credited with five and one shared Bf 109s destroyed, one shared probably destroyed and five damaged – he had earlier scored two kills in North Africa on Hurricane IIs. Sqn Ldr Gerald Matthews, the new OC of No 145 Sqn and a veteran of both the Battles of France and Britain, also did well during this period, claiming two and two shared destroyed, two probably destroyed and one damaged. Added to his previous successes on Hurricanes, these scores made him an ace.

On 4 November, after two weeks of heavy fighting, Allied troops broke through the German and Italian defences at El Alamein. Thus began a long fighting retreat to the west by Axis forces, which continued almost without pause until they were expelled from Libya early in the New Year. Throughout that time there was relatively little air combat, for the Luftwaffe fighter units were depleted in strength and short of fuel. Meanwhile, the focal point of the action had moved several hundred miles to the east, as described in the next section.

OPERATION *TORCH*

On 8 November 1942, just as the Axis defensive line in Egypt was in the process of collapsing, Allied forces opened a new front in North Africa. Codenamed Operation *Torch*, troops landed at widely separated points in Morocco and Algeria, and as soon as airfields had been secured ashore, RAF and USAAF units flew into them and began operations. The RAF contingent included seven units equipped with Spitfire Vs – Nos 72, 81, 93, 111, 152, 154 and 242 Sqns. Two US fighter units also entered the fray equipped with this type, namely the 31st and 52nd Fighter Groups (FGs).

Now the campaign developed into a race, with Allied troops struggling to build up their strength ashore and advance into Tunisia, while German units moved rapidly into that country to establish defensive positions. When the two sides met there were some fierce initial clashes, then the winter set in and the situation degenerated into a stalemate.

The poor state of the roads in Algeria meant that Allied forces in the east of that country and in Tunisia were often short of supplies. Moreover, few airfields in the area were equipped for all-weather operations, which meant that aircraft often became bogged down following periods of heavy rain. These factors imposed severe restrictions on Allied sortie rates.

The Luftwaffe, by contrast, was better placed during the early part of the campaign. Numerically, it was the weaker force, but its airfields in central Tunisia were better equipped and the arrival of a II./JG 2 with its Fw 190A-4s gave the Germans a measure of technical superiority. As a result, on occasions, the Luftwaffe was able to establish air superiority over the battle area. Yet, for much of that winter poor weather prevented effective air operations being performed by either side.

Early in the new year the weather improved, and the situation swung rapidly in the Allies' favour. Following a vigorous airfield improvement programme, their air forces were able to bring greater strength to bear, and from now until almost the end of the campaign there would be a high rate of air activity, with several sharp actions in which both sides took losses.

At the end of January the first Spitfire IXs became operational in the theatre, providing top cover for the other Allied fighter types. Meanwhile, the tightening Allied air and sea stranglehold on the Axis supply route

Ex-Battle of Britain pilot Wg Cdr Ian Gleed was OC No 244 Wing in Tunisia until he was shot down and killed in action on 16 April 1943. At the time of his death his victory score was 13 and 3 shared destroyed, 4 and 3 shared probably destroyed and 4 damaged (*via Franks*)

Above and left
Mk VB AB502/IR-G was Wg Cdr
Gleed's personal mount during the
spring of 1943. This aircraft had
been delivered to the RAF as long
ago as January 1942, being shipped
to Takoradi the following May.
Gleed was fly it on 16 April 1943
when he was killed in action
(*via Robertson*)

from Italy made it increasingly difficult to move supplies and equipment to Tunisia. Under Operation *Flax*, the Allied air forces launched a major campaign to defeat the airlift of supplies to the Axis forces, and scores of Axis transport aircraft were shot down and the Luftwaffe's carrying capacity drastically reduced. From the beginning of April it was clear that the Axis forces in Tunisia were close to collapse, and on 7 May 1943 they capitulated.

The top scoring Spitfire V pilot over Tunisia was Flt Lt Neville Duke of No 92 Sqn (see Chapter Eight), who was credited with the destruction of 12 enemy aircraft and 1 damaged. Another high scorer in-theatre was Wg Cdr Petrus 'Dutch' Hugo, commanding No 322 Wing (see also Chapter Eight), who destroyed eight machines and had one shared destroyed, plus two probably destroyed.

SPITFIRE Vs FAR AND WIDE

DARWIN

Following a series of Japanese air attacks on targets in the Darwin area in February 1942, and the seeming threat of invasion, the Australian Prime Minister, John Curtin, sent an urgent request to Winston Churchill for Spitfires to defend his country. Fighter Command ordered Nos 54, 452 and 457 Sqns – the last two being Australian-manned units – to prepare for the move overseas. In June 1942 the freighters *Nigerstown* and *Stirling Castle*, carrying the units' personnel and 48 crated Spitfire Vs, left Liverpool bound for Melbourne.

As described in the previous chapter, when the convoy reached Freetown in Sierra Leone, *Nigerstown* and her 42 Spitfires were 'high-jacked' for squadrons in the Middle East, leaving only the 6 Spitfires aboard *Stirling Castle* to reach Australia, along with the squadrons' pilots and groundcrews. The ship put into Melbourne on 13 August, where the crated fighters were assembled at nearby RAAF Laverton. From there the fighters moved to RAAF Richmond, near Sydney, where they were flown hard as relays of pilots strove to regain their flying proficiency.

The next large consignment of Spitfires for Australia – 43 brand new Mk VCs – left Liverpool on 4 August on the freighter *Hoperidge*. This vessel and her cargo docked at Melbourne in the third week in October, and the crated fighters were transported to Laverton for assembly. At the same time No 1 Fighter Wing, RAAF, formed at Richmond, with ex-Desert Air Force ace Wg Cdr Clive Caldwell as Wing Leader. The new Spitfires began to reach the squadrons in useful numbers early in November, and during the next two months the units worked hard preparing for action. All three were based at airfields close to Sydney, No 54 Sqn at Richmond, No 452 at Bankstown and No 457 at Camden.

In January 1943 the wing moved to the Northern Territory, No 54 Sqn going to Darwin on the coast, while Nos 452 and 457 Sqns went to the inland airfields at Strauss and Livingstone respectively. At the time this was a remote corner of Australia, and the airfields were ill-equipped for sustained combat operations. Moreover, the units were at the end of long and tenuous supply lines, and duly suffered from shortages of spare parts.

The early operations revealed a spate of problems, for the Spitfire had never flown in a true tropical environment before. On the ground the aircraft faced a combination of humid and dusty conditions with extremely high temperatures, whilst at high altitude the air temperatures were lower than the Spitfire had previously encountered. Almost immediately there was a resurgence of constant speed unit failures, a problem thought to have been solved two years earlier (see Chapter One). However, the earlier modifications did not cope with the new situation, and in the months that followed a number of Spitfires were lost, or damaged, in crash landings following CSU failures, before a new modification was developed to cure the shortcoming.

Further mechanical problems were caused by the failure of ground-crews back in England to inhibit the fighters' engines before they were crated for the long sea voyage. As a result some aircraft arrived with corrosion of the engine coolant piping, which led to glycol leaks – those so afflicted had to be grounded until the piping was replaced.

On 1 February 1943 No 1 Fighter Wing, RAAF, was declared operational, and it got to fire its guns in anger just five days when two Spitfires of No 54 Sqn scrambled to engage a Mitsubishi Ki-46 'Dinah' reconnais-

sance aircraft of the 70th Independent Flying Chutai. Flt Lt Bob Foster, a Battle of Britain Hurricane veteran who went on to 'make ace' in Australia, caught up with the enemy aircraft and sent it crashing into the sea. Hitherto the fast, high flying, 'Dinahs' had operated with impunity and photographed targets in the area at will. From now on their life would become much more difficult.

The next large-scale Japanese

Above, right and below
Mk VC BS164/DL-K of Sqn Ldr Eric Gibbs, OC No 54 Sqn at Darwin, Northern Territory, in March 1943. Delivered to the RAF in June 1942, this aircraft was shipped to Australia on the freighter SS *Hoperidge*. It arrived in October 1942 and was allocated to No 54 Sqn. Gibbs flew this aircraft during all of the sorties for which he made claims, his first being for a Mitsubishi A6M 'Zeke' fighter destroyed on 2 March 1943. When he ended his scoring run just over four months later his tally stood at 5 and 1 shared destroyed and 5 damaged. This Spitfire was transferred to the RAAF in November 1943, but suffered severe damage when it collided in flight with another aircraft in January 1944 and was subsequently written off

attack, and the first to encounter Spitfires, was staged on 2 March when nine Mitsubishi G4M 'Betty' bombers of the Navy's 753rd Kokutai, escorted by twenty-one Mitsubishi A6M 'Zeke' fighters of the 202nd Kokutai, ran in to attack Coomali. These highly-experienced Japanese units were operating from Lautem, in Timor, and 12 Spitfires each from Nos 54 and 457 Sqns, plus Wg Cdr Caldwell and his wingman, scrambled to engage the raiders. On that day the ground control was far from perfect, however, and several Spitfires failed to engage the enemy force at all.

When those Spitfires that did meet the enemy attempted to join combat at high altitude, a new problem emerged. Due to the combination of high temperature and high humidity on the ground, and very low temperatures at altitude, the cannon in a number of the Allied fighters froze up and refused to fire.

Like the engagements in the Battle of Britain, the actions over Australia were characterised by heavy overclaiming on both sides. In a combat involving a large number of aircraft, such overclaiming was to be expected, and on that day the defenders claimed two A6Ms and a Nakajima B5N 'Kate' single-engined bomber destroyed, plus a further B5N damaged. From Japanese records we know that no B5Ns took part in the action, and these aircraft were almost certainly A6Ms misidentified. The Japanese claimed the destruction of three defending fighters, which they reported as 'P-39s' and 'Buffalos' – in fact neither side lost any aircraft during the encounter!

On 7 March four aircraft of No 457 Sqn scrambled to engage a Ki 46 'Dinah' plotted near Bathurst Island, and shot it down into the sea. The next large-scale Japanese incursion took place eight days later when nineteen G4Ms of the 753rd Kokutai, escorted by twenty-six A6Ms fighters from the 202nd Kokutai, attacked Darwin. Twenty-seven Spitfires took off to engage, and the action developed into a fierce dogfight around the bombers. The defenders claimed nine attackers destroyed, four probably destroyed and six damaged for the loss of four Spitfires and two pilots killed. We now know that eight G4Ms returned with battle damage but only one A6M was lost. The raiders claimed the destruction of 11 defending fighters and the probable destruction of 5 more – bombs hit the US Army HQ building in Darwin, rail lines and oil storage tanks.

Groundcrewmen push a Mk VC into its camouflaged dispersal point amongst the Darwin scrub following its return from a coastal patrol

A Mk VC of No 54 Sqn taxies away from of its dispersal at Darwin in preparation for take-off

Mk VCs of No 54 Sqn are photographed airborne over Darwin whilst on patrol (*via Robertson*)

Another lull in air activity then followed, the Japanese next returning in strength on 2 May. The raiding force, drawn from the same units as before, comprised 18 G4Ms and an escort of 26 A6Ms. Some 33 Spitfires scrambled to engage the intruders, but five had to return early due to technical failures. The dogfight around the bombers developed into a running battle which continued for some way out to sea, the defenders claiming seven enemy aircraft destroyed, four probably destroyed and seven damaged. Five Spitfires were lost, or probably lost, to enemy action. Although seven G4Ms and seven A6Ms suffered damage, *all of the raiders regained their base.*

After breaking off the action several defending pilots ran into difficulties. Having flown for long periods at high throttle settings, four Spitfires suffered engine or CSU failures, whilst five more ran out of fuel, with one crashing into the sea and four force-landing. Altogether, 14 Spitfires failed to return from the engagement and three pilots were posted missing. Of the Spitfires that force-landed, one was later recovered intact, three were stripped for spare parts and one was written off.

Even on the basis of the claimed victories, it had not been a good performance by the wing, and afterwards Gen Douglas MacArthur's headquarters added to the blow when it released an official communiqué stating that Spitfires had engaged Japanese bombers and escorts attacking Darwin, but had suffered 'heavy casualties' in the process. The statement attributed some of the losses to adverse winds, which were said to have

Mk VC ES307/UP-X of No 79 Sqn, RAAF, operating from an airfield in New Guinea. The all-white tail was an identification feature requested by the US Fifth Air Force, the main operator in the theatre, and applied from September 1943

carried the Spitfires out to sea. The communiqué made headline news in Australian newspapers. Editorials spoke of 'a serious reverse', and some questioned whether the Spitfire was a match for the 'Zeke' in combat. The report on the adverse weather conditions also received prominence, although it was untrue. The Met record for the area on that day gives the wind at 15,000 ft from the east-north-east at about 20 mph – if anything, it had assisted the defenders during their return flights.

The next encounter over northern Australia took place on 9 May when nine A6Ms again from the 202nd Kokutai carried out a strafing attack on Millingimbi airfield. No 457 Sqn had a detachment based at the airfield, and five Spitfires took off to engage the Japanese fighters. The defenders claimed two A6Ms destroyed and one probably destroyed, and one Spitfire was damaged beyond repair when it crash landed – one A6M was lost in the encounter, and another crash landed on its return flight.

Part of a batch of 143 Spitfire Vs pictured at Abadan, Iran, in April 1943 ready for delivery to the Soviet Air Force (*via Robertson*)

On 17 May Flt Sgt Ross Stagg of No 452 Sqn – one of those posted missing after the 2 May action – unexpectedly turned up at his airfield. During the action he suffered a CSU failure and was forced to bail out of his aircraft, coming down in the sea. He duly boarded his dinghy and paddled ashore at Fog Bay, but once on dry land he had to spend the next two weeks trying to find a way out of the huge area of salt flats behind the shore line.

The Japanese returned to Millingimbi on 28 May, this time with nine G4Ms of the 753rd Kokutai and seven A6Ms from the 202nd Kokutai. Six Spitfires took off to engage the raiders, claiming three bombers shot down for the loss of two Spitfires, but actual Japanese losses were two G4Ms shot down and a third that crash landed near its base. It was the first time the Darwin Spitfires had destroyed any of the bombers! The attacking crews claimed the destruction of four Spitfires.

There followed a two-week lull in action until 17 June, when a Ki 46 'Dinah' ran through the area on a high altitude reconnaissance mission. No fewer than 42 Spitfires took off to engage the intruder, but after a lengthy chase out to sea, the latter escaped.

The next attack on Darwin came three days later, and it differed from those previously mentioned in that it was delivered by Japanese Army aircraft. The bomber force comprised 18 Nakajima Ki 49 'Helens' of the 61st Sentai and 9 Kawasaki Ki 48 'Lillys' of the 76th Sentai, escorted by 22 Nakajima Ki 43 'Oscars' of the 59th Sentai. Two Ki 46 'Dinahs' accompanied the force to conduct post-raid reconnaissance.

This Mk VB was one of those delivered to the Soviet Air Force early in 1943, and it is seen at an exhibition of equipment later in the war. The loop antenna mounted above the rear fuselage belonged to the RPK 10M homing system. The antenna was fixed athwartships, so the pilot could take a bearing only when he was flying towards or away for the beacon (*via Guest*)

Forty-six Spitfires scrambled to engage the raiders, whose attack began with a high altitude bombing run by Ki 49s on Winnellie airfield, followed a few minutes later by low altitude bombing and strafing attacks on Winnellie and Darwin airfields by the Ki 48s. The defenders claimed nine bombers and five fighters destroyed, and eight bombers and two fighters damaged. Three Spitfires were lost, one of whose pilots was saved. Only one Ki

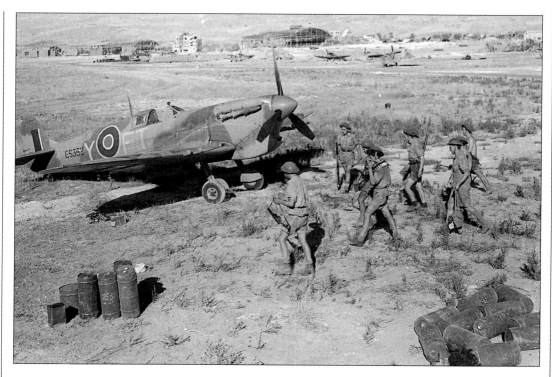

Once the RAF needed to move fighter squadrons into a newly acquired beachhead or an area close to the battle front, its servicing commando units proved invaluable. These men were trained to carry out first-line servicing tasks, and were equipped to defend themselves if necessary. This photo shows a Mk VC of No 43 Sqn with men of a servicing commando at the newly captured airfield at Comiso, Sicily, in July 1943 (*via Robertson*)

49 and a Ki 43 had been actually downed, whilst a further Ki 49 and two Ki 48s forced landed near their base with battle damage. The attackers claimed nine Spitfires destroyed and six probably destroyed.

Eight days later the Japanese Navy returned to Darwin, this time with nine G4Ms and twenty-seven A6Ms. Forty-two Spitfires took off to engage the raiders, and claimed four fighters destroyed and two bombers probably destroyed, for the loss of two Spitfires damaged in crash landings. We now know that all the raiders returned to Lautem, though a damaged bomber crashed on landing. Another G4M and three A6Ms suffered damage.

On 30 June the two Navy kokutais attacked Fenton airfield, home of the USAAF's 380th Bomb Group, whose B-24s had been raiding targets in Japanese-held territory. Some 23 G4Ms and 27 A6Ms took part in the attack, which destroyed 3 B-24s and damaged 7 more. Thirty-eight Spitfires took off to counter the incursion, claiming seven enemy aircraft destroyed, five probably destroyed and eleven damaged in return for the loss of five Spitfires. Two more Spitfires were lost due to engine failures. The sole Japanese loss was a G4M, which suffered battle damage and crash landed near its base. The Japanese crews claimed 16 Spitfires destroyed and 3 probably destroyed.

Six days later Japanese Navy planes returned to Fenton. Twenty-one G4Ms, flying in three shallow 'vics' of seven in each, ran in with an escort of twenty-five A6Ms. Thirty-six Spitfires scrambled to engage the raiders and claimed nine destroyed, three probably destroyed and four damaged. Six Spitfires were lost in combat, and two more crashed following engine failures. Actual Japanese losses were two G4Ms, plus two more which crash-landed with battle damage, and two A6Ms damaged. The raiders claimed 14 Spitfires destroyed and 3 probably destroyed.

By now several of the Spitfires were in poor condition, and the after-action report by No 54 Sqn OC, Sqn Ldr Eric Gibbs (who gained 5½ kills with No 1 Wing), gives an interesting insight into the problems facing the defenders;

'Chiefly owing to the deplorable state of so many of our aircraft, for which no replacements have been forthcoming for months past, we were able to muster only seven Spitfires in the initial attack. Of the

Mk LF VB EP689/UF-X of No 601 Sqn, pictured at Panchino or Lentini West in Sicily in July 1943. This aircraft was often flown by the unit's commander, Sqn Ldr Stanislaw Skalski, the first Polish officer to command a British squadron. At the end of the war Skalski's victory score was at least 21 destroyed, 1 probably destroyed and 5 damaged (*via Jarrett*)

remaining four which were scrambled to intercept, one left the formation before the attack with a severe Glycol leak and subsequently force-landed, and three were unable to keep up . . . We lost two aircraft. Both pilots safe.'

That was the last daylight raid on Darwin, although there would still be some sizeable incursions against other targets in the area – on the night of 13/14 August, for example, an estimated force of nine bombers raided Darwin, although they caused little damage.

On 17 August three Ki 46s flew through the area to conduct a pre-strike reconnaissance for the next attack, and a highly successful interception by Spitfires of Nos 452 and 457 Sqns resulted in all of the high flying 'Dinahs' being shot down. Later that same day a single Ki 46 from the 202nd Sentai was engaged by Wg Cdr Caldwell (in Mk VB JL394) over the ocean to the north-west of Darwin. The aircraft was quickly despatched by the multiple ace, this victory being his 27th, and last, individual kill of the war – eight of these had been claimed whilst leading No 1 Wing.

Nearly four weeks elapsed before the Ki 46s next ventured into the area, and when they did they brought some friends. On 13 September three 'Dinahs' of the 70th Independent Chutai ran in to photograph targets, with thirty-six A6Ms of the 202nd Kokutai providing top-cover! Forty-

Mk VC of the 307th FS/31st FG is seen at Ponte Olivio, Sicily, in August 1943

Mk Vs of the 308th FS/31st FG taxy out for an operation from their base in Italy in 1943 (*via Ethell*)

eight Spitfires took off to engage the intruders, but as they climbed into position to intercept the escorts 'bounced' the defenders and shot three of them down. In the dogfight that followed the Spitfires claimed five Japanese fighters destroyed, two probably destroyed and seven damaged. The A6M pilots stated that they had downed 13 Spitfires and probably destroyed a further 5 'assorted fighters'. The raider's actual loss was one A6M.

On 26 September Japanese Army bombers attacked the Drysdale River Mission airfield, some 21 Ki 48 'Lillys' of the 75th Sentai, escorted by an equal number of Navy A6Ms, hitting the target. No 452 Sqn scrambled Spitfires to engage the raiders, but they failed to make contact – two defending fighters suffered mechanical failures and crashed, killing their respective pilots.

There was a further lull in operations, and the next major raid was on the night of 11/12 November when eight G4Ms of the 753rd Kokutai attacked Fenton. Flg Off Jack Smithson took off to engage, and duly claimed the destruction of two bombers, although only one GM4 was actually lost that night. It was nevertheless a heavy blow for the Japanese unit, as one of the crew members of the stricken 'Betty' was the executive commanding officer of the kokutai, Cdr M Horii.

That was the last occasion on which bombs fell on mainland Australia. Some published accounts have stated that the heavy losses inflicted by the Spitfires forced the raiders to cease their attacks on Australia, but new research makes it clear that this was not the case. In fact, during the series of attacks Japanese losses were remarkably light. The raids only ended when they did because the battle for the Solomon Islands was going badly for the Japanese, and the experienced combat units were required else-where.

For the reasons outlined in this chapter, the Spitfire V failed to defeat the attacks on northern Australia. By the time its failings became known, and the reports reached Supermarine and were duly acted upon, the raids were almost over. The Mk V's successor in- theatre, the Mk VIII, was by then in full production and it incorporated several modifications designed to overcome the problems encountered over Darwin. The new variant would go on to operate successfully in the South Pacific area.

SOVIET SPITFIRES

At the end of 1942 the Soviet government requested that a batch of Spit-fires be included in the military aid package supplied by the western

Allies, so in March 1943 a total of 143 Spitfire Vs arrived in crates at the port of Basra, in Iraq. Staff at the RAF maintenance unit at Shaibah assembled and test flew the fighters, and then handed them over to the Soviet Air Force, whose pilots flew them to the 'Motherland' via Iran. These Spitfires had their VHF radios replaced with the old TR 9 HF sets, with wire aerials between the mast and the tail – at that time the Soviet Air Force did not use VHF radios.

Some of the Spitfires went to the 36th Fighter Aviation Regiment, which moved to Baku on the Caspian Sea to re-equip with the fighter – soon afterwards the unit received coveted 'Guards' status and became the 57th Guards Fighter Aviation Regiment. That spring the regiment took part in heavy air fighting on the southern front over the north coast of the Black Sea, flying Spitfires until the end of June, when it was withdrawn to re-equip with Soviet-built fighters.

Little hard information is available on other Soviet Air Force units that operated Spitfire Vs, although the 821st Air Defence Regiment and the 236th Air Defence Division have been mentioned in this context (see Osprey volume *Aircraft of the Aces 15 Soviet Aces of World War 2* for more details).

SICILY AND ITALY

By the beginning of July 1943 the Allied preparations for the invasion of Sicily were almost complete. Although several units had re-equipped with the more powerful Mk VIIIs and IXs earlier in the year, the Mk V still remained the most numerous Spitfire variant serving in that theatre. For example, on Malta, three out of the five Spitfire fighter squadrons (Nos 185, 229 and 1435) operated the older variant, whilst in North-West Africa ten squadrons (Nos 43, 72, 92, 152, 232, 243, 242, 417, 601 and 1 SAAF) out of fifteen flew Mk Vs. In addition, the USAAF's 31st and 52nd FGs, each the equivalent to an RAF wing, operated a mixture of Mk Vs and IXs. Also committed to support the invasion were three squadrons of Mk Vs serving in the tactical reconnaissance role, and two more operating as fighter-bombers.

On 10 July Allied troops stormed ashore on Sicily and established bridgeheads. On the first day the airfield at Pachino, on the extreme

Mk VCs of No 451 Sqn, RAAF, are seen at El Daba, in Egypt, during the latter part of 1943

southern tip of the island, was captured. The landing ground had been ploughed up by escaping Axis forces to prevent its use, but men of Royal Engineers quickly levelled the surface and an RAF servicing commando made preparations to receive aircraft. Three days later No 244 Wing with its five squadrons of Spitfires (including Nos 92, 417, 601 and 1 SAAF with Mk Vs) moved into the airfield and began operations.

By 15 August, after much heavy fighting, the whole of Sicily was in Allied hands. On 8 September Italy surrendered, and the following day Allied forces landed at Salerno, south of Naples. It was the start of the long, slow, advance northwards up the 'leg' of the country, and in the months that followed more squadrons exchanged their Mk Vs for later Spitfire variants. By the spring of 1944 few Mk Vs remained in frontline service in the theatre.

SOUTH-EAST ASIA

In August 1943 the first batch of Spitfire fighters – Mk VCs – arrived in India. Three Hurricane units (Nos 607, 615 and 136 Sqns in that order) pulled back to Alipore, near Calcutta, to re-equip and re-train with the new fighter. In November Nos 607 and 615 Sqns re-deployed to airfields close to the battle area in Burma, at Nidania and Chittagong respectively. As had been the case over northern Australia, the first to feel the impact of the higher performance fighters were the Ki-46 reconnaissance aircraft that made regular incursions into Allied territory. During the month following their deployment the Spitfires shot down four 'Dinahs'.

On 31 December Royal Navy warships carried out a bombardment of Japanese positions on the Arakan coast. Fourteen Mitsubishi Ki 21 'Sally' bombers, with an escort of about fifteen Ki 43 'Oscar' fighters, ran in to attack the vessels, but No 136 Sqn was ready for them and scrambled twelve Spitfires waiting at readiness at Ramu, in Burma. The Spitfires broke through the screen of escorting fighters to engage the bombers and claimed the destruction of 13 Ki 21s for the loss of a solitary aircraft. However, in light of the new information that has become available on the air actions over Australia, there is reason to treat these claims with some reserve.

In January 1944 the Spitfires engaged 'Oscars' conducting sweeps through the battle area, claiming more than 20 for a cost 4 Spitfires. Following these actions, the level of Japanese air activity in the theatre fell markedly.

Despite the encouraging start, the Spitfire V's operational career in South-East Asia did not last long, for in February 1944 two squadrons arrived in-theatre equipped with Spitfire VIIIs. In March No 607 Sqn converted to the newer variant, followed soon afterwards by the two remaining Mk V squadrons. After replacement, the older fighters performed second-line tasks in the Far East.

Mk VC MA383 was photographed at Dum Dum, Calcutta, in October 1943. It is believed that this machine later served with No 136 Sqn at Baigachi, in Burma, and was flown in action by Sqn Ldr Alexander Constantine, who finished the war with a score of 3 destroyed, 3 probables and 2 damaged – all achieved in January/February 1944 with the Mk VC. This aircraft was struck off charge in July 1944 (*via Thomas*)

TOP SPITFIRE Mk V ACES

This chapter gives the biographies for 12 of the top scoring aces who flew the Spitfire V, listed in order of the number of enemy aircraft credited destroyed to them whilst flying this variant. The headline rank was the highest rank that each pilot attained during World War 2.

FLT LT GEORGE BEURLING

Born in Montreal, Canada, in 1921, George Beurling came to the United Kingdom and joined the RAF in September 1940. After completing his flying training, he was posted in the spring of 1942 to the Spitfire V-equipped No 41 Sqn as a sergeant. While with the unit, he claimed his first two victories – Fw 190s – off the French coast in May.

The following month he flew to Malta as part of Operation *Salient*, and on his arrival Beurling was assigned to No 249 Sqn at Takali. He quickly dedicated himself to improving his skills as an air fighter (particularly in the field of deflection shooting), thus drastically improving his chances of survival in the deadly skies over the embattled island. Beurling proved to be a complex, maverick, character who did not smoke or drink and was not given to swearing – indeed, his prime expletive to anything or anyone unusual was 'Screwball', and this duly became his nickname. In July 1942 the Axis air forces launched a series of all-out attacks on the island, and in the desperate actions that resulted Beurling was in his element. That month he was credited with 15 enemy aircraft destroyed (all German or Italian fighters) and six damaged, a remarkably high rate of scoring. The following month he was commissioned as a pilot officer. October saw a resumption of large-scale Axis air raids on Malta, and in a particularly fierce action on the 14th, Beurling was credited with the destruction of a Ju 88 and two Bf 109s before being wounded in the heel by a cannon splinter and forced to bail out of his aircraft (BR173/D) into the sea, from where he was soon rescued. Following the award of the DSO, he was flown out of the island later that same month and returned to the United Kingdom for treatment and rehabilitation.

Beurling then transferred to the RCAF, returning to operations in the autumn of 1943 flying Mk IXs firstly with No 403 and then with

Flt Lt George Beurling built up the greater part of his score while flying with No 249 Sqn at Takali, Malta, in 1942. A Canadian, 'Screwball' Beurling was the highest scoring pilot in the Mk V, and at the end of the war his victory score stood at 31 and 1 shared destroyed and 9 damaged – all except two of his claims for aircraft destroyed were made while he was flying Spitfire Vs

No 412 Sqn – during this time he added two more Fw 190 kills to his score. Despite his undoubted talent as an air fighter, his refusal to accept authority made him many enemies among his superiors, and there is little doubt that during this period it was only his distinguished combat record that saved him from a court martial. In April 1944 he returned to Canada, and following further disciplinary problems was allowed to resign his commission and retire from the service in October of that same year.

Outside the air force, Beurling proved no better at coping with the demands of civilian life, and for the next three years he drifted from job to job. Then, in the spring of 1948 he accepted an offer to fly with the embryo air force formed by the new state of Israel. His first task was to ferry a Norduyn Norseman light transport to the state, but on 20 May, after taking off from Rome, the aircraft he was flying blew up and crashed, killing both him and his co-pilot – sabotage was suspected but never proven.

At the end of the war Beurling's victory score stood at 31 and 1 shared destroyed, and 9 damaged, all except two of which were made while flying the Spitfire V. This easily made him the most successful pilot on this variant.

AIR COMMODORE JAMES RANKIN

Born in Portobello, Edinburgh, in 1913, James Rankin joined the RAF in 1935 and received a commission. After a spell with the Fleet Air Arm he became a flying instructor, and in June 1940 was serving with No 5 OTU as a flight lieutenant. Early in 1941 he was promoted to squadron leader rank and seconded to No 64 Sqn (flying Spitfire IIs) for a short time to gain operational experience – he scored two damaged and a one-third of a kill during his short time with the unit. Rankin then took command of No 92 Sqn as it was re-equipping with Spitfire Vs, this unit being the first to receive the new variant. During the year he built up a steady score of victories, and in September was promoted to wing commander and appointed OC of the Biggin Hill Wing.

The most effective fighter leaders are those that not only score victories themselves, but also help and encourage junior pilots to emulate their feats. Sgt Jim Rosser was a new pilot with No 72 Sqn when he was invited to fly as wingman to Rankin during a 'Circus' operation. Once over France, the latter sighted a lone Bf 109 and manoeuvred the pair into an attacking position up-sun of the enemy. Rankin then called on the R/T 'Jimmy, there's a nice fat one down there. You have a go. I'll guard your tail'. Rosser did as he was bid and chalked up an easy victory. On their return the young pilot was 'cock-a-hoop' at his feat, and it was typical of Rankin that he confirmed the claim, but remained silent about how it was really achieved.

Between December 1941 and April 1942 Rankin held a staff post at HQ Fighter Command, then returned to Biggin Hill for a second tour leading the wing. In 1943 he commanded No 15 Fighter Wing in the newly formed 2nd Tactical Air Force – when that unit was disbanded he assumed command of No 125 Wing and led this during the Normandy invasion.

By war's end he held the rank of air commodore, but he reverted to

Sqn Ldr James Rankin was one of the top-scoring pilots with the Mk V. He took command of No 92 Sqn early in 1941 as it completed re-equipping with the new variant, and proceeded to build up a steady score of victories. In September he was promoted to wing commander and appointed OC Biggin Hill Wing. At the end of the war his victory score was 17 and 5 shared destroyed, 3 and 2 shared probably destroyed and 16 and 3 shared damaged (*via Franks*)

group captain and retained that rank until he retired from the service in 1958. His wartime score was 17 and 5 shared destroyed, 3 and 2 shared probably destroyed and 16 and 3 shared damaged. Except for 1 shared destroyed and 1 and 2 shared damaged, all these victories were secured while flying Spitfire Vs. James Rankin died some years ago.

SQN LDR ADRIAN GOLDSMITH

Born in New South Wales, Australia, in 1921, Adrian 'Tim' Goldsmith joined the RAAF in 1940, and after completing his flying training, he was posted to No 234 Sqn in September 1941 as a sergeant. In February 1942 he was posted to Malta, being one of a group of reinforcement pilots flown in by Sunderland flying boat. During the month that followed he flew Hurricanes with Nos 126, 242 and 185 Sqns, before returning to No 126, which, in the meantime, had re-equipped with Spitfires. When his tour on Malta ended in July 1942 he was credited with 11 victories, and had been commissioned as a pilot officer. On his return to the UK Goldsmith instructed for a time at No 53 OTU, before returning to Australia to join No 452 Sqn as part of No 1 Fighter Wing, RAAF, at Darwin. He claimed two Japanese bombers and two fighters destroyed, and a fighter damaged, during the battles off the northern Australian coast in 1943. In April 1944 he became a flying instructor and saw no further action.

Adrian Goldsmith was credited with 16 and 1 shared enemy aircraft destroyed, 2 probably destroyed, and 7 damaged. Except for one aircraft damaged (in a Hurricane II), all his claims were made while flying Spitfire Vs. Goldsmith died in 1961.

SQN LDR NEVILLE DUKE

Born in Tunbridge, Kent, Neville Duke joined the RAF in 1940, and in April of the following year he joined No 92 Sqn at Biggin Hill – soon after it re-equipped with Spitfire Vs. By the end of August his score was two enemy aircraft destroyed and two damaged (all Bf 109Fs), and he was quickly picked out as a talented novice and, on occasion, chosen to fly as wingman to the commander of the Biggin Hill Wing, Wg Cdr 'Sailor' Malan.

In November 1941 Duke was posted to No 112 Sqn in North Africa, flying firstly the Tomahawk and then the Kittyhawk. In the months that followed he rapidly built up his score, and by the end of February 1942 it stood at eight destroyed, three probably destroyed and four damaged. From then until November, Duke served as an instructor at the fighter School at El Ballal in Egypt, before returning to No 92 Sqn as a flight commander. Still operating Spitfire Vs, the unit was now based in Tunisia, and Duke continued to build up his score to the point where, at the completion of his tour in June, he had added a further 14 victories to his total. He was then promoted to squadron leader and spent a further period at a training unit at Abu Sueir, in Egypt, as its Chief Flying Instructor.

In March 1944 he assumed command of No 145 Sqn, flying Spitfire VIIIs, in Italy, and by September Duke had become the top scoring RAF fighter pilot in the Mediterranean theatre.

He returned to the United Kingdom in October 1944 and was allocated to Hawker Aircraft Ltd as a production test pilot. After the war he

Flt Lt Neville Duke flew Spitfire Vs with No 92 Sqn soon after the variant entered service, then went to the Middle East where he built his score flying Tomahawks and Kittyhawks. In November 1942 he returned to No 92 Sqn, still operating Spitfire Vs but now based in Tunisia. Duke continued to score victories, and when his tour ended in June he had added a further 14 kills to his total. Later he took command of No 145 Sqn with Spitfire VIIIs, and went on to become the top-scoring pilot of the Mediterranean theatre. After the war he joined Hawker Aircraft Ltd as a test pilot, and carried out much of the early test flying of the company's Hunter jet fighter

attended a course at the Empire Test Pilots School, then joined the RAF High Speed Flight in June 1946. In 1948 he left the service and returned to Hawker to work as a test pilot where, in 1951, he became Chief Test Pilot. Whilst in that post he carried out much of the early test flying of the company's successful Hunter jet fighter.

At the end of the war Neville Duke was credited with 26 and 2 shared enemy aircraft destroyed, 1 probably destroyed, and 6 damaged. Of those, 14 destroyed and 3 damaged were achieved while flying the Spitfire V.

SQN LDR HENRY WALLACE MCLEOD

Born in Regina, Canada, in 1915, 'Wally' McLeod joined the RCAF in September 1940, and after completing his training was posted to No 132 Sqn as a pilot officer in July 1941. He spent brief periods with Nos 485, 602 and 411 Sqns over the ensuing 12 months, and claiming a solitary Bf 109 as having been damaged during this time. In June 1942 he flew to Malta as part of Operation *Style*, and on arrival he was allocated to No 603 Sqn. In the following month he became one of the founder members of No 1435 Sqn and was appointed a flight commander at the end of August. During the October 'Blitz' on Malta McLeod became one of the top scoring pilots, before he leaving the island at the end of the month 'tour expired'. He returned to Canada where he instructed for a time at an OTU, but early in 1944 McLeod returned to the UK and took command of No 443 Sqn. In the months that followed he continued to add to his score until he was shot down and killed near Nijmegen on 27 September in a Mk IX, having being bounced by nine Bf 109Gs.

At the time of his death McLeod was credited with the destruction of 21 enemy aircraft, 3 probably destroyed, and 12 and one shared damaged. Of these, 13 destroyed, 2 probably destroyed and 11 and 1 shared damaged were secured while flying Spitfire Vs.

LT COL JEAN-FRANCOIS DEMOZAY

Born in Nantes, France, in 1916, Jean-Francois Demozay was called up for military service in 1938 but was invalided out one month later. He duly returned to his job as an airline pilot, and when the war began Demozay volunteered for service in the air force. Given a commission and tasked with performing non-combatant duties, he was seconded to the RAF in France as an interpreter, where he served with the Hurricane-equipped No 1 Sqn.

With the fall of France he escaped to the United Kingdom in an abandoned Bristol Bombay transport aircraft, and in the confusion that followed in the wake of the Dunkirk evacuation, he had no difficulty in passing himself off as a fighter pilot. Demozay was accepted into the RAF and sent to No 5 OTU to convert on to Hurricanes, then rejoined No 1 Sqn as a pilot in the autumn of 1940 and scored three kills with the unit in the spring of 1941. After a brief spell with No 242 Sqn (where added two Bf 109s to his tally), which was also flying Hurricane IIs, Demozay moved to the Spitfire V-equipped No 91 Sqn in July. After scoring heavily with this unit (ten Bf 109s destroyed), he moved to No 11 Group on a staff appointment early in the New Year, but returned to No 91 Sqn in June as commander. Demozay scored a further four kills against the Fw

After flying Hurricanes with Nos 1 and 242 Sqns, Flt Lt Jean-Francois Demozay joined No 91 Sqn, which eqipped with Spitfire Vs, in July 1941. The Frenchman went on to become one of the top scorers on this variant (*via Franks*)

190 on his second tour with this unit, and at the end of the year promoted to wing commander. In early 1943 he went to North Africa to set up a flying school for French pilots, and in April of the following year he was appointed to the French Air Ministry in London and sent on a special mission to the USSR. Following the invasion he formed the Groupement 'Patrie', a French unit to conduct air operations against German troops cut off in ports by-passed by the Allied advance. After the war he was appointed deputy commander of flying training schools in France, but was killed in an air accident in December 1945.

By war's end his total victory score was 18 destroyed, 2 probably destroyed and 4 damaged, and of these 13 were destroyed, 2 probably destroyed and 3 damaged while flying Spitfire Vs.

WG CDR EVAN MACKIE

Born in Ortorohanga, New Zealand, in 1917, Evan 'Rosie' Mackie joined the RNZAF in January 1941. Upon the completion of his training some 12 months later, he was sent to the UK and posted to No 485 'New Zealand' Sqn as a pilot Officer to commence his career flying the Spitfire V. Whilst with the unit he opned his tally with a half-share in a Bf 109E, plus was awarded probable kill over a Fw 190. In March 1943 he joined No 243 Sqn in Tunisia, and was appointed flight commander the follow month. From then on his score built up rapidly, and by the time he assumed command of the unit in June, Mackie had added 6¹/₂ kills to his European successes. He led the unit during the invasion of Sicily and the campaign in Italy that followed, downing a further six aircraft. In November he became OC No 92 Sqn, flying Spitfire VIIIs, but early in 1944 he returned to the United Kingdom and converted onto Tempests. Mackie scored 6¹/₂ kills with the new Hawker fighter, rising to the rank of wing commander and given charge of No 122 Wing.

By war's end his final victory score had risen to 20 and 3 shared destroyed, 2 probably destroyed and 10 and 1 shared damaged. Of that total 12 and 3 shared destroyed, 2 probably destroyed and 7 and 1 shared damaged were secured while flying Spitfire Vs. Evan Mackie died in the 1980s.

GRP CAPT PETRUS HUGO

Born in Pampoenpoort, South Africa, in 1917, Petrus 'Dutch' Hugo joined the RAF early in 1939, and after completing his flying training was posted to the Gladiator II-equipped No 615 Sqn. He fought with distinction with unit (now flying Hurricanes) firstly in France and then during the Battle of Britain, scoring 4¹/₆ confirmed and two unconfirmed kills. In 1941 the squadron converted to cannon-armed Hurricanes IICs, and Hugo took part in several attacks on enemy shipping and land targets – a quarter-share in a He 59 was his only success during this period.

In November 1941 he assumed command of No 41 Sqn, equipped with Spitfire Vs, and the following April he was appointed commander of the Tangmere Wing, but his time in that post was short, however, because at the end of the month he was shot down and wounded by a Fw 190. In July 1942 he took over the leadership of the Hornchurch Wing, a position he held for a few months before being promoted that autumn to

Sqn Ldr Evan Mackie, a New Zealander, commanded No 243 Sqn from June to November 1943, during which time it was involved in the invasion of Sicily and the early stages of the campaign in Italy. At the end of the war his victory score was 20 and 3 shared destroyed, 2 probably destroyed and 10 and 1 shared damaged. Of that total 12 and 3 shared destroyed, 2 probably destroyed and 7 and 1 shared damaged were secured while flying Spitfire Vs (*via Franks*)

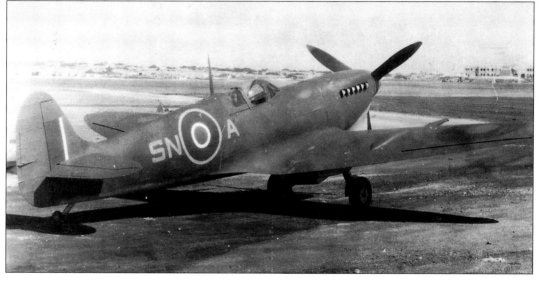

Evan Mackie with his Mk VC, JK715, pictured at Hal Far, Malta, in June 1943 when he commanded No 243 Sqn. Mackie flew this aircraft exclusively between the end of April and mid-September, when he was credited with the destruction of 8 enemy aircraft destroyed, 1 probably destroyed and 4 shared damaged. That makes JK715 one of the most successful, if not *the* most successful, of the Mk Vs in action. Note the non-standard Mk IX-type exhaust stubs, which added about 7 mph to the speed of this aircraft (*via Shores*)

group captain rank – he had scored three kills, one probable and four damaged whilst flying Spitifres on the Channel front. Hugo was then appointed commander of No 322 Wing in late 1942, leading the Spitfire force with great success (he was personally credited with $8^{1}/2$ kills and 2 probables in a little over four weeks of fighting) during the invasion of north-west Africa. In March 1943 he moved to a staff appointment at HQ North West African Coastal Air Force, but by June he had returned to No 322 Wing, and duly led it until it was disbanded in November 1944, adding two more victories to his tally. For the rest of the war Hugo held staff appointments, and he finally parted company with the the RAF in 1950.

At the end of the war his total victory score was 17 and 3 shared destroyed, 3 probably destroyed and 7 damaged. Of those 12 and 1 shared destroyed, 3 probably destroyed and 5 damaged were claimed while flying Spitfire Vs. Petrus Hugo died in 1986.

FLT LT JOHN YARRA

Born in Queensland, Australia, in 1921, Jack 'Slim' Yarra joined the RAAF in October 1940, and after completing his flying training in Canada, he was posted in October 1941 to No 232 Sqn as a sergeant. Soon afterwards he moved to No 64 Sqn, but early in 1942, having attained the rank of flight sergeant, Yarra was posted to Malta and flew to the island as part of Operation *Picket II* on 21 March. Initially he was allocated to No 249 Sqn, but after a few sorties he moved to No 185 Sqn, where he flew Hurricane IIs until Spitfires became available. With this unit he built up a sizeable victory score, and received his commission. Yarra's tour on the island ended in mid-July and he returned to the UK where, following a spell of leave, he was posted to No 453 Sqn as a flight commander. He was killed in action on 10 December 1942 during an attack on enemy ships off the Dutch coast.

At the time of his death Jack Yarra was credited with 12 enemy aircraft destroyed, 2 probably destroyed and 6 damaged. All of them were secured during his time in Malta, and all bar a probably destroyed while flying Spitfire Vs.

FLG OFF PATRICK SCHADE

Born in Malaya of British parents, Patrick 'Paddy' Shade joined the RAF in 1940 and was posted to No 501 Sqn, flying Hurricanes, as a sergeant early in 1941. In July he moved to No 54 Sqn, then flying Spitfire Vs, but failed to gain any victories during his time on the Channel front. Early in 1942 he was posted to Malta, flying into to the island in March during Operation *Picket II* to join No 126 Sqn as a flight sergeant. Faced with innumerable opponents, Schade built up his victory score to the point that when he left the island 'tour expired' in August, he was then Malta's top scoring pilot. Upon his return to the United Kingdom, he was posted to No 62 OTU to instruct, receiving his commission soon after his arrival at the training unit.

In 1943 Schade served for a time with the Air Fighting Development Unit, before being posted to No 91 Sqn with Spitfire XIIs and later XIVs. From June 1944 the unit was heavily engaged during the V1 bombardment of London, and Schade was credited with the destruction of two flying bombs. At the end of July he was attempting to intercept another V1 in bad weather when his Spitfire XIV collided with a Tempest and he crashed to his death.

At the time of his death Patrick Schade was credited with the destruction of 12 enemy aircraft, 2 probably destroyed and 2 damaged, plus a pair of V1s destroyed. Apart from the the latter, all his victories were secured over Malta while flying Spitfire Vs.

FLT LT RAYMOND HESSELYN

Born in Invercargill, New Zealand, in 1921, Raymond Hesselyn initially joined the Territorial Army before transferring to the RNZAF in 1940. After completing his training in New Zealand in 1941 he joined No 234 Sqn as a sergeant, but subsequently gained no aerial kills. Early in 1942

Petrus 'Dutch' Hugo, a South African, pictured at the time he flew Hurricanes with No 615 Sqn during the Battle of Britain. Later he took command of No 41 Sqn with Spitfire Vs, then the Tangmere Wing and later still No 322 Wing in Algeria and Tunisia. He was one of the top-scoring pilots on the Mk V, with 12 and 1 shared destroyed, 3 probably destroyed and 5 damaged. At the end of the war his total victory score was 17 and 3 shared destroyed, 3 probably destroyed and 7 damaged.

Hesselyn was posted to Malta, and he flew onto the island on 7 March as part of Operation *Spotter* – the first such deployment of Spitfires. On arrival he was assigned to No 249 Sqn at Takali, and he immediately began to to build up his victory score. By mid-July his tour on the island ended and he returned to the UK, having downed 12 aircraft, had 1 listed as a probable and damaged 6 others.

 Hesselyn spent six months on second line duties before being posted to No 501 Sqn, then onto No 277 Air-Sea Rescue Sqn – whilst with the latter unit he damaged a Fw 190 over the Channel in an 'ancient' Spitfire Mk II on 22 June 1943! In September 1943 he was posted to No 222 Sqn as a flight commander, and the following year he added $6^{1}/_{2}$ kills to his score flying Mk IXs. This promising wartime career came to a sudden end in October 1943 when he was shot down by a Bf 109G and taken prisoner – he had managed to down at least one (he claimed three after the war) of his attackers before being forced to bail out with leg wounds. On his return from captivity he accepted a permanent commission in the RAF and became a squadron leader at HQ Fighter Command.

At the time of his capture Hesselyn's victory score stood at 18 enemy aircraft destroyed and 1 shared destroyed, 2 probably destroyed and 7 damaged. Of that total 12 destroyed, 1 probably destroyed and 6 damaged were secured while flying Spitfire Vs from Malta. He died in 1963.

GRP CAPT GEORGE GILROY

Born in Edinburgh, Scotland, in 1914, George 'Sheep' Gilroy was a sheep farmer when he joined No 603 Auxiliary Sqn in 1938. By the time the unit mobilised in September 1939 it had been issued with Spitfires, and over the following month Gilroy took part in some of the first RAF fighter engagements of the war. For example, on 16 October 1939 he was credited with a share in a He 111 destroyed over the Firth of Forth, which was was followed by two more such victories in January and March 1940. Gilroy went on to fly with No 603 Sqn throughout the Battle of Britain and the months that followed it, building up a sizeable score in the process – three and seven shared kills and four damaged.

In July 1941 he was promoted to squadron leader and appointed commander of No 609 Sqn. During his time with this unit he downed a further four fighters and damaged a fifth whilst flying Spitfire VBs. In May 1942 he moved to a staff appointment, before achieving wing commander rank in November and assuming command of No 324 Wing in Tunisia, which was equipped with Spitfire Vs. He remained in that post through the invasions of Sicily and Italy, continually adding to his score – 7 and 3 shared destroyed, 2 shared probables and 2 and 2 shared damaged.

In November 1943 he was promoted to group captain and appointed to command RAF Wittering. Although he left the RAF at war's end to resume his career as a sheep farmer, Gilroy later rejoined No 603 Sqn, Auxiliary Air Force, as a squadron leader and was appointed commander of the unit.

His final score was 14 enemy aircraft destroyed and 10 shared destroyed, 2 shared probably destroyed, and 5 and 4 shared damaged. Of that total 11 of the destroyed, 2 shared probably destroyed and 5 and 3 shared of those damaged were attained while flying Spitfire Vs.

APPENDICES

Specifications

Spitfire VB W3134, tested May 1941

Type: single-seat air superiority fighter

Armament: two Hispano 20 mm cannon with 60 rounds per gun, four Browning .303-in machine guns with 350 rounds per gun

Powerplant: one Rolls-Royce Merlin 45 engine rated at 1185 bhp for take-off. Emergency combat power, five minutes maximum, 1515 bhp at 11,000 ft at +16 lbs boost

Dimensions: span 36 ft 10 in, length 29 ft 11 in, wing area 242 sq ft

Weight: loaded, 6525 lbs

Performance: maximum speed 371 mph at 20,000 ft, climb to 20,000 ft in 8 mins 24 secs, service ceiling (estimated) 37,500 ft

Notes: this was the first production Spitfire VB built as such, with full operational equipment. The performance figures were taken with the carburettor snow guard removed. With the guard in place the speed was reduced by about 6 mph

Spitfire VA (Tropicalised) X4922, tested early 1942

(Note: details given only where they differ from those for the aircraft above)

Powerplant: one Rolls-Royce Merlin 46 engine rated at 1100 bhp for take-off. Emergency combat power, five minutes maximum, 1415 bhp at 14,000 ft at +16 lbs boost

Weight: loaded, 6440 lbs

Performance: maximum speed 363 mph at 20,800 ft, climb to 20,000 ft in 7 min 48 secs, service ceiling (estimated) 38,500 ft

Notes: aircraft fitted with tropical air filter under nose. Armament was not fitted during these tests, ballast equivalent to eight .303-in machine guns carried in lieu and the gun ports sealed over

Spitfire LF VB W3228, tested early 1943

(Note: details given only where they differ from those for the aircraft above)

Type: single-seat low altitude air superiority fighter

Armament: two Hispano 20 mm cannon with 60 rounds per gun, four Browning .303-in machine guns with 350 rounds per gun

Powerplant: one Rolls-Royce Merlin 50M engine, rated at 1230 bhp for take-off. Emergency combat power setting, five minutes maximum, 1585 bhp at 2750 ft at +18 lbs boost

Weight: loaded, 6450 lbs

Performance: maximum speed $350\frac{1}{2}$ mph at 5900 ft, climb to 8000 ft in 1 min 45 sec, service ceiling 35,700 ft

Notes: this aircraft was fitted with standard wings. In service most LF VBs had clipped wings, which added about 5 mph to their maximum speed below 10,000 ft

Spitfire Mk VB versus Fw 190A

In June 1942 the RAF captured a Fw 190 in flyable condition, and during the weeks that followed the Air Fighting Development Unit at Duxford conducted methodical one-versus-one comparative flight trials against each of the available Allied fighter types, including the Spitfire VB. Since first encountering the Fw 190 in action some ten months earlier, Fighter Command's pilots had come to appreciate that they faced a formidable opponent. Now, the trials revealed just how formidable! Excerpts from the official report on the trials are given below;

'The Fw 190 was compared with a Spitfire VB from an operational squadron for speed and all-round manoeuvrability at heights up to 25,000 feet. The Fw 190 is superior in speed at all heights, and the approximate differences are as follows:

At 2000 ft (610 m) the Fw 190 is 25-30 mph (40-48 km/h) faster than the Spitfire VB.

At 3000 ft (915 m) the Fw 190 is 30-35 mph (48-56 km/h) faster than the Spitfire VB.

At 5000 ft (1525 m) the Fw 190 is 25 mph faster than the Spitfire VB.

At 9000 ft (2744 m) the Fw 190 is 25-30 mph faster than the Spitfire VB.

At 15,000 ft (4573 m) the Fw 190 is 20 mph (32 km/h) faster than the Spitfire VB.

At 18,000 ft (5488 m) the Fw 190 is 20 mph faster than the Spitfire VB.

At 21,000 ft the Fw 190 (6400 m) is 20-25 mph faster than the Spitfire VB.

Climb: the climb of the Fw 190 is superior to that of the Spitfire VB at all heights. The best speeds for climbing are approximately the same, but the angle of the Fw 190 is considerably steeper. Under maximum continuous climbing conditions the climb of the Fw 190 is about 450 ft/min better up to 25,000 ft.

Dive: comparative dives between the two aircraft have shown that the Fw 190 can leave the Spitfire with ease, particularly during the initial stages.

Manoeuvrability: the manoeuvrability of the Fw 190 is better than that of the Spitfire VB except in turning circles, when the Spitfire can quite easily out-turn it. The Fw 190 has better acceleration under all conditions of flight and this must obviously be most useful during combat. When the FW 190 was in a turn and was attacked by the Spitfire, the superior rate of roll enabled it to flick into a diving turn in the opposition direction. The pilot of the Spitfire found great difficulty in following this manoeuvre and even when prepared for it, was seldom able to allow the correct deflection. A dive from this manoeuvre enabled the Fw 190 to draw away from the Spitfire which was then forced to break off the attack.

The above trials have shown that the Spitfire VB must cruise at high speed when in an area where enemy fighters can be expected. It will then, in addition to lessening the chances of being successfully "bounced", have a better chance of catching the Fw 190, particularly if it has the advantage of surprise.'

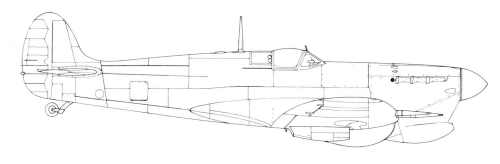

**All drawings on this page are of
a Spitfire Mk VC at 1/72nd scale**

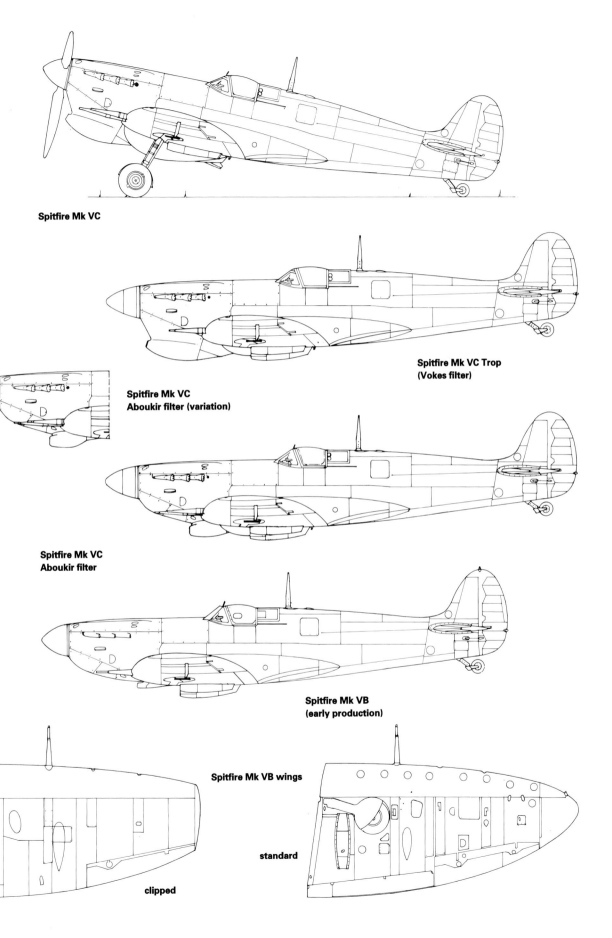

Spitfire Mk VC

Spitfire Mk VC Trop
(Vokes filter)

Spitfire Mk VC
Aboukir filter (variation)

Spitfire Mk VC
Aboukir filter

Spitfire Mk VB
(early production)

Spitfire Mk VB wings

standard

clipped

COLOUR PLATES

1

Mk VA W3185/D-B *Lord Lloyd I* of Wg Cdr Douglas Bader, OC Tangmere Wing, Tangmere, August 1941

This aircraft was delivered new to No 145 Sqn on 30 June 1941, and after short periods with both Nos 41 and 616 Sqns at Tangmere, it became Douglas Bader's personal mount at the end of July. Indeed, he was flying it on 9 August 1941 when shot down whilst engaging Bf 109Fs of II./JG 26 over France – Bader was credited with one fighter destroyed and one probable prior to W3185's demise. At the time of his capture Bader's victory score was 20 and 4 shared destroyed, 6 and 1 shared probably destroyed and 11 damaged – the claims of 9 August were the sole successes enjoyed by the pilot with the Mk V.

2

Mk VB RS-T of Wg Cdr Robert Stanford Tuck, OC Biggin Hill Wing, Biggin Hill, February 1942

Although the serial number appears to have been painted over in all the photographs that have survived of this aircraft, it is thought to be BL336, which was delivered new to No 124 Sqn (one of the wing's constituent units) on 28 November 1941. This Mk VB was being flown by Tuck as part of a two-aircraft 'Rhubarb' against the Hesdin distillery, inland from Le Touquet, on 28 January 1942. Having strafed the giant vats, he then turned his sights on a train, but was hit by flak from an AA battery on the outskirts of Boulogne that had also been attacked by the two Spitfires. Crash landing alongside his target, Tuck was quickly taken prisoner. At the time of his capture Tuck was credited with 27 and 2 shared destroyed, 6 probably destroyed and 6 and 1 shared damaged, although none of these claims were achieved with the Mk V, as he was shot down just weeks after assuming command of the Biggin Hill Wing.

3

Mk VB W3561/M-B of Wg Cdr Minden Blake, OC Portreath Wing, Portreath, summer 1942

Although this aircraft was delivered to the RAF in July 1941, it only entered frontline service with No 313 Sqn in October of that year. After two months with the Czech-manned unit, it was transferred to No 130 Sqn, where it eventually became wing leader Minden Blake's personal Spitfire. The New Zealand ace (a veteran of the Battle of Britain) was flying this aircraft on 19 August 1942 when he was credited with the destruction of an Fw 190 near the Dieppe landing beaches. However, shortly after claiming his first kill in over a year, Blake was himself shot down into the Channel and taken prisoner. At the time of its loss it is likely that this Spitfire was carrying the special *Jubilee* markings, which comprised four white stripes around the engine cowling. Blake's score stood at 10 and 3 shared destroyed, and 1 shared damaged when made a PoW, although only his final kill was achieved in a Mk V.

4

Mk VB AB502/IR-G of Wg Cdr Ian Gleed, OC No 244 Wing, Goubrine South, 16 April 1943

This aircraft was delivered to the RAF in January 1942 and shipped to Takoradi where, upon its arrival in May, it was fitted with an Aboukir filter prior to being issued to No 244 Wing. It

became Ian Gleed's personal aircraft in early March 1943, the wing leader flying it on at least 35 missions over the Tunisian battlefront in the month prior to his death – during this time he used it to down one Bf 109G and damage two others. On 16 April 1943 he was shot down and killed whilst attempting to attack Axis transport aircraft over the Tunisian coast, falling victim to the latters' fighter escort (Bf 109Gs of I./JG 77 and Fw 190As of II./JG 2). At the time of his death, Gleed's score stood at 13 and 3 shared destroyed, 4 and 3 shared probably destroyed and 4 damaged – of this total, 3 destroyed, 1 and 2 shared probables and 3 damaged were gained while flying the Mk V.

5

Mk VC BR498/PP-H of Wg Cdr Peter Prosser Hanks, OC Luqa Wing, Luqa, October 1942

This aircraft was delivered to the RAF in June 1942 and shipped to Gibraltar the following month. It was then loaded aboard HMS *Eagle* and delivered to Malta during one of the July reinforcement operations – either *Pinpoint* or *Insect*. Once on the island it served with Nos 126, 1435 and 185 Sqns, before ending its career with the Malta Conversion Flight. Its pilot in October 1942 was Hurricane ace Peter Prosser Hanks, who had seen combat with No 1 Sqn in France prior to the Battle of Britain. Posted to Malta as wing leader just prior to the October 'Blitz', Hanks employed this Mk V to great effect during the month, downing three Bf 109s and a Ju 88 cofimred, as well as damaging a further three aircraft. BR498 remained in service until struck off charge in September 1945. By war's end Hanks's score was 13 and 1 confirmed, 3 shared probably destroyed and 6 damaged, of which 4 confirmed, 1 and 1 shared probable and 6 damaged were claimed in the Mk V.

6

Mk VC BS234 (A58-95)/CRC of Wg Cdr Clive Caldwell, OC No 1 Fighter Wing, RAAF, Livingstone, March 1943

Delivered to the RAF in August 1942, this aircraft was shipped to Australia on the freighter SS *Raranga*, arriving in November 1942. After re-assembly at RAAF Laverton, the fighter was assigned to No 457 Sqn, which was one of the component units of No 1 Fighter Wing. Whilst in the Northern Territory, the aircraft was used for a time by Australia's leading ace of World War 2, Clive Caldwell, although none of the eight kills he claimed between March and August 1943 were achieved in this aircraft. Although Caldwell left the wing in September to take up a posting as Chief Flying Instructor at No 2 OTU, 'CRC' remained with No 457 Sqn until August 1944, when it too was sent to No 2 OTU. Like virtually all surviving Spitfires in Australia in 1945, A58-95 was declared surplus to requirements after VJ-Day and reduced to components in November of that year. At the end of the war Caldwell's score was 27 and 3 shared destroyed, 6 probably destroyed and 15 damaged, of which 8 of the destroyed had fallen to the guns of a Mk V.

7

Mk VC BS164 (A58-63)/DL-K of Sqn Ldr Eric Gibbs, OC No 54 Sqn, Darwin, July 1943

Delivered to the RAF in June 1942, this aircraft was shipped to Australia on the freighter SS *Hoperidge*, arriving in October 1942. Following re-assembly, it was allocated to No 54 Sqn, and more specifically the unit's new OC, Sqn Ldr Eric Gibbs. An ex-Hudson pilot with Coastal Command's No 608 Sqn,

Gibbs seemed an unusual choice to lead a single-engine fighter squadron, but his lack of experience in this role failed to impede him in his daunting task. and he duly became No 54 Sqn's leading ace in Australia with five and one shared kills and five damaged. All these claims (his only confirmed victories of the war) were scored in this particular aircraft between March and July 1943, and consisted of Zero fighters and 'Betty' bombers. Following its service with the RAF unit, BS164 was transferred to the RAAF (and No 452 Sqn) in November 1943, being given the code A58-63. Soon after its change of owner-ship the Spitfire was written off in the New Year in a mid-air collision with A58-214 (LZ845) near Strauss airfield.

8
Mk VB SH-Z *Atchashikar* of Sqn Ldr Wilfred Duncan-Smith, OC No 64 Sqn, Hornchurch, May 1942

Although the serial has been painted over in photographs of this Mk VB, it is thought to be BM476, which was delivered new to the unit in April 1942. Spitfire ace Duncan-Smith had assumed command of No 64 Sqn just the month before, and chose this aircraft as his own after having initially flown BL787. Duncan-Smith scored one kill, one probable and one damaged (all Fw 190s) in this machine during May/June, before his unit became the first to transition to Spitfire Mk IXs in July. This air-craft went on to see further frontline action with Nos 154, 165, 122, 234, 303 and 26 Sqns, before passing into OTU service in 1944 and finally being written off in a crash landing at Hawarden following an engine fire on 28 April 1945. As BM476's most successful pilot, Wilfred Duncan-Smith finished the war with 17 and 2 shared destroyed, 6 and 2 shared proba-bly destroyed and 8 damaged – of this total, 8 destroyed, 5 probables and 2 damaged were scored with the Mk V.

9
Mk VB BM361/XR-C of Sqn Ldr Chesley Peterson, OC No 71 'Eagle' Sqn, Gravesend, August 1942

This aircraft was delivered new to No 453 Sqn in April 1942, and went on to serve briefly with both Nos 41 and 72 Sqns before being transferred to No 71 'Eagle' Sqn on 2 August. Assigned to unit commander Chesley 'Pete' Peterson, the air-craft lasted just 17 days with the Americans, as it was downed by return fire from a Ju 88 off Dieppe on 19 August – Peterson had earlier destroyed a Junkers bomber, and damaged a sec-ond, during this action-packed sortie. Quickly picked up by a rescue launch, the pilot had to endure a strafing attack by an Fw 190 before finally reaching the safety of an English port. By war's end Peterson's score stood at 8 destroyed, 3 probably destroyed and 6 damaged, of which 6 destroyed, 2 probables and 6 damaged came while flying Mk Vs.

10
Mk VC AB216/DL-Z *Nigeria Oyo Province* of Sqn Ldr Robert Oxspring, OC No 91 Sqn, Hawkinge, May 1942

This aircraft was delivered new to the unit in March 1942, but its regular pilot, Battle of Britain Spitfire ace 'Bobby' Oxspring, failed to add to his tally with it during its time with No 91 Sqn. The Spitfire was damaged in operations in June 1943, and after repairs had been affected, it went to the Aircraft & Armaments Experimental Establishment, where it was fitted with a glider towing attachment. Once modified, the Spitfire was used in tests that saw it tow various glider types in order to assess the

feasibility of transporting groundcrews in this way during rapid deployment operations. The aircraft was written off in February 1945 following an engine fire in flight. Oxspring, who finished the war as a wing commander, had a tally of 13 and 1 shared destroyed, 2 probably destroyed and 13 damaged – 3 destroy-ed, 2 probables and 7 damaged were achieved on Mk Vs.

11
Mk VB R6923/QJ-S of Flg Off Alan Wright, No 92 Sqn, Biggin Hill, May 1941

This aircraft first flew in July 1940, and was amongst the initial batch of cannon-armed Mk IBs that saw brief service with No 19 Sqn during the Battle of Britain. When the problems with the cannon installation on this variant were finally solved, the Spitfire had its four outer .303-in machine guns restored and it was reissued to a frontline unit – No 92 Sqn – in the winter of 1940-41. It soon became the personal aircraft of Battle of Britain ace Alan Wright (throughout his operational career his aircraft carried the identification letter 'S'), and he used it to damage two Bf 109s on a high altitude sweep off the English coast on 13 March 1941. Early the following month the aircraft went to Rolls-Royce for conversion to Mk VB standard, after which it returned to No 92 Sqn. Wright continued to fly this air-craft until it was downed by a II./JG 26 Bf 109 on 21 June whilst being flown by a Sgt Ashton as part of Circus No 17 – the latter claimed a Bf 109 prior to baling out of R6923. By war's end Allan Wright's score was 11 and 3 shared destroyed, 5 probably destroyed and 7 damaged, of which 1 shared destroyed and 2 probables were claimed with the Mk V.

12
Mk VB W3312/QJ-J *Moonraker* of Sqn Ldr James Rankin, OC No 92 Sqn, Biggin Hill, August 1941

This Spitfire was delivered new to No 92 Sqn on 20 June 1941, and it was immediately 'acquired' by the unit's boss, 'Jamie' Rankin, who scored 11 and 1 shared kills, 1 probable and 4 damaged (all against fighters) with it between mid-June and late October – his first two kills in W3312 were scored within 24 hours of the aircraft arriving on the squadron! He even con-tinued to fly *Moonraker* after he had been made OC of the Biggin Hill Wing in September of that year. Rankin gave up the post in December 1941, and the battle-seasoned Spitfire was passed to the recently arrived No 124 Sqn. It was damaged on ops in April 1942, and following repairs, was issued to No 65 Sqn, with whom it was written off in September of that same year. At the end of the war Rankin's score was 17 and 5 shared destroyed, 3 and 3 shared probably destroyed and 16 and 3 shared damaged – except for 1 shared destroyed and 1 and 2 shared damaged, all these kills were secured flying Spitfire Vs.

13
Mk VB JU-H of Sgt Peter Durnford, No 111 Sqn, Debden, December 1941

This aircraft carries the nocturnal camouflage scheme briefly worn by Spitfire Vs of No 111 Sqn during the winter of 1941/42 whilst part of the hastily-assembled nightfighter force tasked with protecting London – the RAF believed at the time that the Luftwaffe would resume their large-scale night raids of exactly 12 months before. This scheme totally obliterated any distin-guishing serials, although it is believed that JU-H was W3848, a presentation Mk VB (christened *Travancore II*) that had been delivered new to No 111 Sqn in September 1941. In February 1942 the Spitfires were repainted in normal day-fighter colours, and this particular aircraft went on to serve with Nos 41, 122 and 222 Sqns, before being relegated to second line duties in late 1943 – it survived the war and was finally struck off charge in December 1945. Peter Durnford finally opened his score on 30 April 1942 when he shot down an Fw 190 on a day sweep over France. He moved to No 124 Sqn the following month, and continued on ops until 19 November when he was shot down by flak on his 137 mission and eventually taken prisoner. When captured Durnford's score stood at five destroyed and one damaged – three of these were gained on Mk Vs.

14

Mk VB BP850/F of Flt Sgt Patrick Schade, No 126 Sqn, Takali April 1942

This aircraft was delivered to the RAF in February 1942 and shipped to Gibraltar, where it was loaded aboard HMS Eagle as part of Operation Picket II. It arrived on Malta on 29 March, as did its future pilot, 'Paddy' Schade. Both joined No 126 Sqn, and on 23 April the pair combined to destroy a Ju 87 as it pulled off its target, plus shared in the destruction of a second Stuka. BP850 was written off 24 hours later when RCAF pilot Sgt E A Crist was forced to crash land after the fighter had developed a glycol leak following combat with Ju 87s. 'Paddy' Schade enjoyed a much longer stay on Malta than BP850, going on to become one of the island's highest scoring pilots with at least 12 destroyed, 2 probably destroyed and 2 damaged – all in Mk Vs. He was killed in action flying a Spitfire XIV with No 91 Sqn in July 1944, having added two V1 flying bombs to his total.

15

Mk VC BR112/X of Sgt Claude Weaver of No 185 Sqn, Krendi, September 1942

Delivered to the RAF in March 1942, this aircraft was one of 47 embarked on USS Wasp in Glasgow as part of Operation Calendar and flown off the carrier to Luqa on 20 April 1942. Once on the island it was issued to No 249 Sqn, where the aircraft was heavily used throughout the summer until being passed on to No 185 Sqn. Here, it was flown by numerous pilots, including American Malta ace Claude Weaver, who had joined the RCAF prior to his country entering the war. BR112 was finally lost during a squadron sweep over Sicilian airfields on 9 September with Weaver at the controls – but not before the extrovert American had destroyed a MC 202 just prior to being shot down himself by another Macchi fighter. With his Spitfire hit in the cooling system, Weaver crashed on the beach and was taken prisoner. Following the Italian armistice he escaped from captivity, returned to England and resumed operations flying Spitfire IXs with No 403 Sqn. Weaver quickly got back into the swing of things over France by downing two Fw 190s, but he was killed on 28 January 1944 when he fell victim to a 6./JG 26 Fw 190. At the time of his death Weaver's tally was 12 and 1 shared destroyed and 3 probably destroyed – all but the final two Fw 190s were scored with the Mk V.

16

Mk VB AD233/ZD-F West Borneo I of Sqn Ldr Richard Milne, OC No 222 Sqn, North Weald, March 1942

Delivered new to the unit in October 1941, this Mk V eventually became Battle of Britain ace 'Dickie' Milne's personal air-

craft in March 1942. When the latter left the unit at the end of his tour in May of that year, the Spitfire was taken over by his Polish replacement, Sqn Ldr Jerzy Jankiewicz, who had also see action during the Battle of Britain. Unfortunately the new OC lasted just a matter of days, as he was shot down and killed by a I./JG 26 Fw 190 whilst flying AD233 on a 'Rodeo' to Ostend on the morning of 25 May 1942. 'Dickie' Milne, however, survived the war (he did spend the last two-and-a-half years of it as a PoW, however), having scored 14 and 1 shared destroyed, 1 probably destroyed and 11 damaged – 3 destroyed, 1 probable and two damaged were claimed with the Mk V.

17

Mk VC JK715/SN-A of Sqn Ldr Evan Mackie, OC No 243 Sqn, Hal Far, June 1943

Delivered to the RAF in February 1943, this aircraft was shipped to the Middle East the following month and issued to No 243 Sqn in April, where it became Evan Mackie's personal aircraft. Between then and mid-September, Kiwi Mackie was credited with the destruction of 8 enemy aircraft, 1 probably destroyed and 4 shared damaged, all whilst flying this machine – a record which makes JK715 one of the most successful, if not the most successful, Mk V to see service with the RAF. Note the aircraft's non-standard Spitfire IX-type exhaust stubs, which Mackie obtained specifically for this fighter. JK715 later flew with the USAAF in North Africa and then No 208 Sqn in the tactical recce role, before being struck off charge in April 1945. Mackie ended the war with 20 and 3 shared destroyed, 2 probably destroyed and 10 and 1 shared damaged, of which 12 and 3 shared destroyed, 2 probably destroyed and 7 and 1 shared damaged were secured while flying Mk Vs.

18

Mk VB AB262/GN-B of Flg Off Robert McNair, No 249 Sqn, Takali, March 1942

Following this aircraft's delivery to the RAF in January 1942, it was allocated to Operation Spotter – the first delivery of Spitfires to Malta, via HMS Eagle, on 7 March 1942. Canadian-born 'Buck' McNair had flown into the island aboard a Sunderland on 17 February, and then basically sat around awaiting the arrival of the first Spitfires – he had seen action over France with No 411 Sqn the previous autumn. McNair and AB262 linked up on 18 March to damage a Bf 109 that had been attempting to intercept a Maryland bomber returning from an anti-convoy raid, but this was to be the Canadian's only success with the aircraft. The Spitfire was subsequently damaged in a raid whilst undergoing repairs in a Kalafram workshop the following month and eventually struck off charge. By war's end McNair's victory tally was 16 destroyed, 5 probably destroyed and 14 damaged – 7 destroyed, 5 probables and 9 damaged were scored in the Mk V.

19

Mk VC BR323/S of Sgt George Beurling, No 249 Sqn, Takali, July 1942

Delivered to the RAF in May 1942, this aircraft took off from HMS Eagle and flew to Luqa during one of the two reinforcement operations in June – Style or Salient. Once on the island it was issued as a combat replacement to No 249 Sqn and allocated the single letter code 'S'. Like numerous other Spitfires flown into Malta that year, BR323 was to enjoy only a brief

career, during which time its was flown predominantly by leading ace 'Screwball' Beurling. His first successes with 'S' came
on 6 July when he was credited with the destruction of two
MC 202s and a Bf 109 (this triple-kill haul gave him ace status),
as well as damaging a Cant Z 1007 bomber. The Spitfire had
suffered damage during the two sorties flown by the Canadian
pilot that day, however, and it was grounded for repairs until 10
July, when Beurling used it to destroy an MC 202 and a Bf 109.
Two days later the aircraft was written off after suffering further damage in action whilst being flown by another pilot. At
the end of the war Beurling's victory score was 31 and 1
shared destroyed and 9 damaged, all except two of which
were achieved while flying the Spitfire V.

20

Mk VB EP706/T-L of Sqn Ldr Maurice Stephens, No 249 Sqn, Takali, October 1942

This aircraft was delivered to the RAF in July 1942, and was
then probably flown to Malta from HMS *Furious* during one of
the August reinforcement operations – either *Bellows* or
Baritone. It had seen two months of service with No 249 Sqn
by the time it was flown in combat by newly-arrived supernu-
mary squadron leader 'Mike' Stephens (a Battle of France ace).
His first successes over Malta came in this aircraft on 10
October when he was credited with one Bf 109 probably
destroyed and another damaged – Stephens went on to firstly
command No 229 Sqn and then the Hal Far Wing. EP706 soldiered on with No 249 Sqn until it was lost due to engine failure
on a patrol over the Mediterranean on 3 March 1943. 'Mike'
Stephens's final victory score was at least 17 and 3 shared
destroyed, 1 probably destroyed and 5 damaged, of which 6
and 2 shared destroyed, 1 probable and 4 damaged were
scored in Mk Vs (all over Malta).

21

Mk VB EP340/T-M of Flg Off John McElroy, No 249 Sqn, Takali, October 1942

Delivered to the RAF in June 1942, this aircraft was almost certainly amongst the 30 Spitfires flown to Malta from HMS *Eagle*
during Operation *Insect* on 21 July. Once on the island it was
issued to No 249 Sqn, who used it throughout the summer
and into the autumn of 1942 until it became the 30th victim of
I./JG 53 *Expertan*, Unteroffizier Marian Mazurek, on 15
October – EP340's pilot, Australian Flt Sgt Edwin Hiskens, was
killed in the engagement. Two days prior to its demise, the
Spitfire had been successfully flown by Canadian ace John
McElroy, who had been flying with the unit since his arrival on
the island on 9 June during Operation *Salient*. Engaging the
fourth Axis raid on Malta that day, McElroy had been part of an
eight-aircraft formation put up by No 249 Sqn (which included
the ill-fated Flt Sgt Hiskens) to oppose the 79-strong fighter
and bomber force sent to bomb the island. Five fighters and
two bombers were claimed by the defenders, with McElroy
being credited with a Re 2001 destroyed and a Bf 109 damaged. The Canadian finally returned to UK in December 1942,
and by war's end McElroy's score was 10 and 3 shared destroyed, 1 and 1 shared probably destroyed and 12 damaged, of
which 7 and 2 shared destroyed, 1 and 1 shared probably
destroyed and 11 damaged were claimed in Mk Vs. In 1948/49
he added an Egyptian C 205V and two RAF Spitfire FR 18s to
his tally whilst flying an Israeli Spitfire IX with No 101 Sqn.

22

Mk VB EP829/T-N of Sqn Ldr Joseph Lynch, OC No 249 Sqn, Krendi, April 1943

This aircraft was delivered to the RAF in August 1942 and then
crated up and shipped to Gibraltar, where it arrived the following month. The manner of its delivery to Malta is not recorded,
however, and it could have made the flight direct through the
employment of a 170-gallon ferry tank. Once in the frontline it
was issued to No 249 Sqn, where it was employed with great
success by the unit's American OC, 'Eagle' Squadron veteran
Joseph Lynch, during April 1943. Indeed, the Californian used
it to 'make ace', downing $3^1/2$ Ju 52/3ms (including the 1000th
Axis aircraft destroyed by the defences of Malta on 28 April), a
Ju 88 and a Caproni Ca 313 – little else is known of the history
of this aircraft in the RAF. However, by an ironic twist of fate it
was one of a batch of Spitfires delivered to the Italian Air Force
in 1946, were it was issued with the code MM4069. Moreover
when it reached that service it was allocated to *51° Stormo CT*,
one of the Italian fighter units against which it had almost certainly seen action three years earlier! At the end of the war
Joseph Lynch's victory score stood at 10 and 7 shared
destroyed, 1 probably destroyed and 1 shared damaged, all of
which were achieved with Mk Vs.

23

Mk VB AA853/C-WX (of No 302 'Polish'Sqn) believed flown by Wg Cdr Stefan Witorzenc, OC 1st Polish Fighter Wing, Kirton-in-Lindsey, detached to Heston, Operation *Jubilee*, 19 August 1942

This aircraft was delivered new to the unit in October 1941,
and it is seen here wearing four white stripes painted on the
engine cowling as an RAF identification marking during the
Dieppe landings – it is likely that many other fighter units also
carried the striped markings on that day. This combat veteran
later served with Nos 501, 350 and 322 Sqns before being
destroyed in a mid-air collision with Mk V AR498 (which also
hailed from the Dutch-manned No 322 Sqn) during a 'Jim
Crow' patrol over the Channel from Hawkinge on 11 January
1944. Its pilot during *Jubilee* was Battle of Britain veteran
Stefan Witorzenc, who had flown with the Polish Air Force
prior to reaching England in 1940. Although he failed to add to
his tally with the Mk V, he was already an ace by the time of
the Dieppe operation, having scored 5 and 1 shared destroyed
and two damaged – all on Hurricanes.

24

Mk VC AB174/RF-Q of Plt Off Antoni Glowacki, No 303 'Polish' Sqn, Kirton-in-Lindsey, August 1942

This aircraft was delivered new to the unit at Northolt in March
1942, and was used by Polish Battle of Britain ace 'Toni'
Glowacki during the Dieppe operation, when it almost certainly
carried nose stripes. In that action he was credited with an He
111 shared destroyed and an Fw 190 probably destroyed.
Damaged in a flying accident the following month, it was reissued to training unit upon its repair in early 1943, before again
going into the frontline with No 313 Sqn at Ibsley in October of
that year. In February it was passed to the newly-formed No
442 Sqn at Digby. However, it only remained with the
Canadian-manned unit until new Mk IXs arrived the following
month, after which it was passed to No 56 OTU, where it was
destroyed in a flying accident in early May 1944. 'Toni'

Glowacki's final victory score was 8 and 1 shared destroyed, 3 probably destroyed and 5 damaged, of which 1 shared, 2 probables and 1 damaged were achieved in the Mk V.

25

Mk VB BM144/RF-D of Flt Lt Jan Zumbach, No 303 'Polish' Sqn, Northolt, May 1942

Delivered new to No 303 Sqn at Northolt in March 1942, this Mk VB was issued to Jan Zumbach soon after he returned to his Battle of Britain unit that same month as a flight commander, following a spell instructing. His only success in BM144 came on 27 April when he was credited with the probable destruction of a Fw 190 (from JG 26) near Lille during Circus No 141, the Northolt Wing flying escort cover for 12 Boston bombers of No 107 Sqn tasked with hitting the power station near the French town. The aircraft is shown in the markings it wore in May 1942, just prior to it being passed to fellow Polish-manned unit, No 315 Sqn. Within a few days of it donning the latter's 'PK' codes it suffered minor damage during a combat sortie, but was soon repaired and put back into service. It remained on strength with No 315 Sqn through to October 1943, when it was finally written off in a crash landing following an engine failure in flight. Jan Zumbach survived the war with a victory tally of 12 and 2 shared destroyed, 5 probably destroyed and 1 damaged – 3 and one shared destroyed, 2 probables and 1 damaged were scored with Mk Vs.

26

Mk VB W3718/SZ-S of Flt Lt Stanislaw Skalski, No 316 'Polish' Sqn, Northolt, April 1942

Delivered new to No 306 Sqn in September 1941, this aircraft saw just a few weeks of service with the unit before being transferred to fellow Northolt Wing members No 303 Sqn. It wore this outfit's famous 'RF' codes for a little over three months before moving yet again at the Middlesex fighter base to No 316 Sqn in January 1942. Here, it was flown by numerous pilots including leading Polish ace Stanislaw Skalski who, whilst flying W3718 on 25 April 1942, was credited with damaging an Fw 190 of JG 26. After completing its spell with the Polish wing that summer, the Spitfire went on to serve with Nos 66, 340, 26, and 278 Sqs, before finally being written off in April 1945 whilst serving with No 53 OTU. At the end of the war Skalski's victory score was 21 destroyed, 1 probably destroyed and 5 damaged, 3 destroyed, 1 probable and 1 damaged having been achieved with the Mk V.

27

Mk VB AA758/JH-V *Bazyli Kuick* of Flt Sgt Stanislaw Brzeski, No 317 'Polish' Sqn, Exeter, November 1941

This fighter was delivered new to the unit in October 1941, the Polish-manned squadron having just traded up from Hurricane IIBs to Spitfire Mk VBs at their Exeter base. A veteran fighter pilot who had tasted success both with the Polish Air Force in September 1939 and the RAF's No 249 Sqn in early 1941, Stanislaw Brzeski quickly exploited the superiority of his new mount over the PZL P XICs and Hurricanes that he had previously flown by downing a Bf 109F and damaging an Fw 190 (both from JG 26) during Circus No 110 on 8 November – he was flying AA758 on this occasion. He later achieved ace status in this aircraft on 25 April 1942 when he downed a Fw 190 (of JG 26) during an early-morning 'Ramrod' on the Dunkirk

docks. Although Brzeski was posted away soon after Dieppe, AA758 remained with the unit until December 1942, when it was passed to No 164 Sqn. It later served with Nos 341 and 340 Sqns, before being issued to a Fleet Air Arm operational conversion unit at Henstridge in May 1944. Brzeski survived the war with a score of 7 and 3 shared destroyed, 4 probably destroyed and 1 damaged, of which 5 and 1 shared destroyed, 2 probables and 1 damaged were gained with the Mk V.

28

Mk VB EN786/FN-T of Flt Lt Kaj Birksted, No 331 'Norwegian' Sqn, North Weald, June 1942

This aircraft was delivered now to the unit at North Weald in June 1942, where it was initially flown with great success by flight commnader Kaj Birksted. A pre-war Danish Air Force pilot, Birksted had completed a tour with No 43 Sqn prior to being posted newly-formed No 331 'Norwegian' Sqn in July 1941. His first combat victories came almost a year later on 19 June 1942 when he was credited with downing an Fw 190, and damaging another (both from II./JG 1) over the Belgian coast. He later gained 1 1/2 kills (Fw 190 and a Bf 109F) in EN786 over Dieppe on 19 August. After seeing much action with No 331 Sqn, this Spitfire was lost on operations on 1 November 1942. By war's end Birksted's victory score stood at 10 and 1 shared destroyed and 5 damaged – 2 and 1 shared destroyed and 1 damaged were achieved on Mk Vs.

29

Mk VB BM372/YO-F of Plt Off Donald Morrison, No 401 'Canadian' Sqn, Gravesend, May 1942

This aircraft was delivered new to the unit at Gravesend in April 1942, being flown by Canadian Don Morrison soon after he had returned from completing the Central Gunnery Course at Wittering. The lessons he had learned were soon called in to practice for on 24 May he used BM372 to damage two Fw 190s during a late evening 'Rodeo' between Hardelot and St Omer. The Spitfire had earlier suffered collision damage after hitting squadronmate AD506 whilst taxying at the Kent base. In December 1942 it was shipped to Iran for delivery to the Soviet Air Force, and its ultimate fate is unknown. Morrison – who lost a leg in combat in November 1942 as a result of injuries inflicted by a cannon shell fired from a Fw 190 of JG 26 – finished the war with a tally of 4 and 3 shared destroyed, 4 and 1 shared probably destroyed and 5 damaged, of which 2 and 2 shared destroyed, 1 and 1 shared probably destroyed and 5 damaged were claimed with the Mk V.

30

LF VB EP120/AE-A of Sqn Ldr Geoffrey Northcott, No 402 'Canadian' Sqn, Merston, August 1943

Delivered new to No 501 Sqn at Ibsley in June 1942, this aircraft was firstly involved in a taxying accident with AB401 of No 118 Sqn a month after its arrival, then damaged in action over Dieppe on 19 August. It then spent seven months with No 19 Sqn, before transferring to No 402 Sqn at Digby in April 1943. The following month it was assigned to newly-arrived Malta veteran, Geoffrey Northcott, who assumed command of the Canadian-manned unit in June. The partnership forged between the two campaigners was immediately successful, and between 27 June and 3 November, Northcott destroyed four Bf 109s (plus damaged a fifth) and three Fw 190s during operations over France and Holland – EP120 is shown here in the markings it wore on 22 August when Northcott downed an Fw 190 over Beaumont-Le-Roger to 'make ace'. Remarkably, this aircraft remained with No 402 Sqn until mid-1944, the fighter then being overhauled and issued to No 53 OTU in October, before becoming an instructional airframe. After serving as a gate guardian, this aircraft was acquired by The Fighter Collection at Duxford in the late 1980s and restored to flying condition in the markings it carried when Geoff Northcott flew it. The latter ended the war with 8 and 1 shared destroyed, 1 probably destroyed and 7 and 1 shared damaged, with all but a solitary damaged claim being scored with the Mk V.

31
Mk AD196/DB-P of Plt Off Henry McLeod, No 411 'Canadian' Sqn, Digby, April 1942
Delivered new to No 71 Sqn at North Weald on the last day of August 1941 as part of the initial batch of Mk Vs issued to the unit, this aircraft was later transferred to No 411 Sqn. Whilst with the Canadians, the fighter was used by 'Wally' McLeod to damage an Fw 190 and a Bf 109 on 15 April 1942, followed by an Fw 190 probable on May Day. He was then posted to Malta, but AD196 soldiered on with 'Ramrods' amd Circuses' until it failed to return from operations on 27 August. By the time he was killed in action in September 1944 flying a Spitfire Mk IX with No 443 Sqn, 'Wally' McLeod's victory score was 21 destroyed, 3 probably destroyed and 12 and 1 shared damaged, and of these, 13 destroyed, 2 probably destroyed and 11 and 1 shared damaged were secured while flying Mk Vs.

32
Mk VB BM205/OU-H *Nova Scotia* of Plt Off Evan Mackie, No 485 'New Zealand' Sqn, Kenley, April 1942
This aircraft was delivered virtually 'fresh from the factory' to the New Zealand-manned unit at Kenley in March 1942, and flown by squadron 'new boy', 'Rosie' Mackie. He scored a probable Fw 190 kill in it over Boulogne on 26 April, which was his last success with No 485 Sqn. BM205 suffered minor combat damage the following day during Circus No 141, but this was soon repaired back at Kenley. The Spitfire later served with Nos 401, 504, 129 and 402 Sqns between October 1943 and July 1944, when it was finally retired from frontline duties to No 53 OTU and eventually struck off charge in May 1945. Although only scoring 1 shared kill and 1 probable with No 485 Sqn, 'Rosie' Mackie's tally had risen to 20 and 3 shared destroyed, 2 probably destroyed and 10 and 1 shared damaged by war's end – 12 and 3 shared destroyed, 2 probably destroyed and 7 and 1 shared damaged were secured while flying Vs.

33
Mk LF VB X4272/SD-J of Flt Lt David Fairbanks, No 501 Sqn, Friston, June 1944
As recounted elsewhere in this account, X4272 had a remarkably long service history, for it first flew in August 1940 as a Mk I and was then fitted with cannon to become a Mk IB – it saw limited service with No 92 Sqn in this less than successful configuration later that year. Early in 1941 it was modified into a Mk VB, and returned to the squadron as one of the first examples of this variant to enter service. The aircraft then went on to serve with No 222 Sqn, before spending time in storage prior to being chosen for conversion to LF Mk VB standard. By 1944

it was serving in the frontline once again, this time with Friston-based No 501 Sqn, and on 8 June 1944 flight commander David 'Foob' Fairbanks (an American who joined the RCAF before his country entered the war) used X4272 to down a Bf 109 and damage another near Le Havre. The aircraft's record card gives no further information on its remaining career, but in August the unit re-equipped with Tempests and it is likely that the weary fighter was passed to an OTU. By war's end Fairbanks score stood at 12 and 1 shared destroyed and 3 damaged, his successes with X4272 being his only with the Mk V.

34
Mk VC BP955/J-1 of Flt Lt Denis Barnham, No 601 Sqn, Luqa, April 1942
Delivered to the RAF on 20 March 1942, this aircraft was allocated to No 601 Sqn and loaded by crane on the aircraft carrier USS *Wasp* at Port Glasgow just weeks later. On 20 April the Spitfire took off from the carrier and flew to Luqa as part of Operation *Calendar* – one of the pilots involved in this operation was Denis Barnham, a flight commander with No 601 Sqn. He flew BP955 into action the very next day, being credited with the probable destruction of a Ju 88 and inflicting damage on a Bf 109. He was forced to crash-land moments after attacking the Junkers bomber after his Spitfire was hit in the engine by enemy fire. Barnham's aircraft was eventually returned to flight status, only to be eventually lost in action near Luqa on 17 October 1942 – its pilot, Sgt Ron Miller of No 229 Sqn, was never found. At the end of the war Barnham's victory score stood at 5 and 1 shared destroyed, 1 probably destroyed and 1 damaged, all of these falling to the guns of Mk Vs.

35
Mk LF VB EP689/UF-X of Sqn Ldr Stanislaw Skalski, OC No 601 Sqn, based at Panchino and Lentini West, July 1943
This aircraft was delivered to the RAF in July 1942 and arrived in the Middle East the following October. It was initially delivered to No 92 Sqn, and remained with the unit until they were posted to Malta in July 1943, when it was passed to No 601 Sqn – this outfit took it with them to Sicily later that month. Legendary ace Stanislaw Skalski assumed command of the unit at about the same time, thus becoming the first Polish officer to command a British squadron in the process, and he often flew this aircraft in combat. EP689 was finally lost on 22 September 1943 when its pilot hit an unspecified obstruction on the ground during a practice strafing attack at Catania.

36.
Mk VB W3238/PR-B *The London Butcher* of Sqn Ldr Michael Robinson, OC No 609 Sqn, Biggin Hill, July 1941
One of the first Mk VBs delivered to 'Biggin on the bump', this newly-built aircraft arrived at the Kent fighter station in May 1941 and was immediately chosen by No 609 Sqn OC, Sqn Ldr 'Mickey' Robinson, as his personal mount. A Battle of Britain ace on Hurricanes, Robinson went on to enjoy even greater success on the Spitfire. Indeed, between 3 and 12 July 1941 he destroyed five Bf 109Fs and damaged four more with *The London Butcher*. The fighter was damaged in a flying accident in September, and after being repaired, it was issued to No 92 Sqn the following month. Its time with the unit was to be brief, however, for it was written off following yet another non-operational crash in December 1941. When 'Mickey' Robinson was

killed in action leading the Tangmere Wing in April 1942, his victory score was 16 destroyed, 4 and 1 shared probably destroyed and 8 and 1 shared damaged – 8 destroyed, 1 probable and 6 damaged were achieved with the Mk V.

37

Mk VB BL584/DW-X of Flt Lt Denis Crowley-Milling of No 610 Sqn, Ludham, July 1942

Delivered new to the unit at Ludham in April 1942, this aircraft briefly served as the personal mount of flight commander Denis Crowley-Milling following his return to the unit after 12 months spent evading capture in occupied Europe. The Spitfire was transferred to No 111 Sqn at Kenley on 16 July and was lost on operations nine days later. By the end of the war Crowley-Milling's victory score was 4 and 1 shared destroyed, 2 probably destroyed and 1 and 1 shared damaged – a shared kill and 2 probables were claimed on the Mk V.

38

Mk VB (serial overpainted – unknown) YQ-A of Sqn Ldr Colin Gray, OC No 616 Sqn, King's Cliff, January 1942

New Zealander Colin Gray's fine career flying Spitfires in combat is described in the two earlier works in this series. His command of No 616 Sqn with Spitfire VBs lasted from September 1941 through to February 1942, and during that time the unit was based in the Midlands, which meant there were few opportunities for Gray to engage the enemy. At the end of the war his total score was 27 and 2 shared destroyed, 6 and 4 shared probably destroyed and 12 damaged, of which 4 destroyed were achieved with the Mk V.

39

Mk VB EN853/AV-D of Maj William Daley, 335th FS/4th FG, USAAF, Debden, October 1942

Although photographic evidence confirms the serial LN853 painted on this aircraft, that number was spurious (it was in a block allocated to Wellington X bombers), and this Spitfire is In fact EN853. Delivered to the RAF in May 1942, it served for a time with No 401 Sqn before moving to No 121 'Eagle' Sqn at Rochford in August 1942. Here, it was flown by flight commander 'Jimmy' Daley, a Texan who had joined the RAF before his country entered the war. Both Daley and this Spitfire were with the unit when it was transferred to the USAAF's Eighth Air Force in September 1942 and renamed the 335th FS/4th FG – Daley took command of the unit in November, then returned to the USA, whilst EN853 was written off during operations in January 1943. Its former pilot returned to combat with the 371st FG in 1944, but was killed when his wingman taxied into his P-47 at a forward landing ground in France on 10 September. Daley's tally then stood at 2 and 1 shared destroyed and 3 damaged, all scored with the Mk V.

40

Mk VC BR114/B of Flg Off George Genders (and other pilots), No 103 Maintenance Unit, Aboukir, September 1942

This aircraft was delivered to the RAF in March 1942, and was then crated up and carried by freighter to Takoradi before flying on to Egypt on the trans-African reinforcement route. At No 103 Maintenance Unit at Aboukir, the aircraft became one of a handful of specially-modified high altitude interceptors built to counter Ju 86P recce aircraft that regular overflew the area. All non-essential equipment was removed including the radio, armour and armament, the aircraft's engine was modified to give a higher increased compression ratio and a four-bladed propeller fitted. The Spitfire was fitted with pointed wing tips and two .5-in machine guns. Later, it was restored to normal Mk VC standard and flown by Nos 601, 451 and 123 Sqns, before being passed to to French Air Force recce unit *CR 2/33*, based in North Africa, in July 1944. Its operational life with the French was to be short, however, for on 1 August it suffered serious flak damage and was written off. As BR114's pilot on many of its high altitude sorties, George Genders, finished the war with a score of 8 and 2 shared destroyed, 2 probables, and 3 and 2 shared damaged, of which 1 and 1 shared destroyed and 2 shared damaged were achieved with the Mk V.

FIGURE PLATES

1

Sqn Ldr M L 'Mickey' Robinson, OC No 609 Sqn, is illustrated wearing his faded RAF officers' Battle Dress, complete with a yellow-painted 1932 Pattern life jacket (whistle attached), at Biggin Hill in mid-1941. Note that he has dispensed with the regulation black tie, choosing instead to leave his bright pale blue shirt undone at the collar. In his right hand is a well-worn Type B helmet, fitted with a Type D (Type 19) oxygen mask and Mk III goggles. Finally, his boots are 1936 Pattern issue.

2

Based at North Weald in September 1941, Flg Off G A 'Gus' Daymond of No 71 'Eagle' Sqn is wearing much the same gear as Robinson, although his Battle Dress is a darker shade of blue due to its 'newness' – note also the 'Eagle Squadron' patch on his shoulder. Daymond's life jacket is of a later interim pattern, his goggles are Mk IVs and his gloves standard issue.

3

Wg Cdr A G 'Sailor' Malan, OC Biggin Hill Wing in mid-1941, is also attired in standard Service Dress, although he is wearing a 'field service' cap. Note the 'South Africa' flashes on his shoulders and turned over thick stockings covering his boot tops

4

Still with the Service Dress theme, Sgt 'Tommy' Rigler (of No 609 Sqn at Biggin Hill in mid-1941) shows the 'other ranks' eagle and rank badge on his right sleeve. Note also that his life jacket is only partly painted.

5

No 92 Sqn's Flt Lt Neville Duke is seen in Tunisia in March 1943 wearing standard RAF issue khaki drill trousers and shirt, over which he has put on his Battle Dress blouse – note his DFC ribbon. On his feet he is wearing suede 'desert boots'.

6

Wg Cdr Clive 'Killer' Caldwell, OC No 1 Fighter Wing, RAAF, is seen in RAAF issue khaki drill shirt and shorts, over which he is wearing a late issue RAF life jacket. His waist webbing is also RAF issue, the pouch and case attached to it supporting a .38 cal service revolver. Caldwell's boots are 1936 Pattern issue, under which he is wearing khaki socks, and although his leather flying helmet is an RAF Type D, his goggles are USAAF B-7s and his oxygen mask is also of American origin.